Cover Issues

Business Interruption

Published by
Cunningham Lindsey United Kingdom
Apex Plaza, Forbury Road, Reading, Berkshire RG1 1AX

First Edition September 2005

British Library Cataloguing-in-Publication Data
A catalogue record for this book is available from the British Library.

ISBN 0-9550848-0-6

Origination by Oakley Design Associates, London SE1
Printed by The Garda Solution, Wickford, Essex

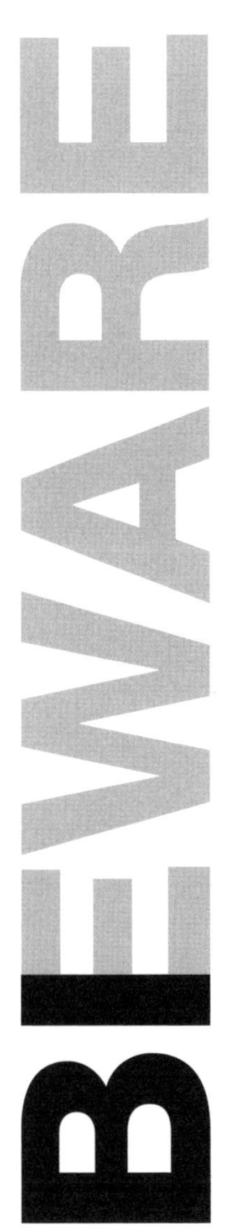

Cover Issues

Business Interruption

Damian Glynn BA(Hons) FCA FCILA

Cunningham Lindsey

Acknowledgements

I am indebted to the number of people that have assisted me in the preparation of this book with technical review and input being received from insurers (claims and underwriting), brokers, solicitors, forensic accountants, loss adjusters and loss assessors. The technical feedback from John Armstrong, Andrew Neill, Bill Padley, John O'Neill and Harry Roberts has been invaluable as has the underlying support dealing with administrative issues from Martin Geyer.

With regards to external feedback, I would like to express my gratitude to Harry Rule (Allianz Cornhill), John Wickham (Norwich Union), Graham Annand (Zurich), Andrea Masters (Zurich), Graeme Drysdale (AXA) and Tom Wood (ACE) who provided feedback from an insurer perspective. Prominent brokers including Ann Stone (SBJ), Peter Franklin (JLT), Paul Hodgson (Towry Law), Alex Finch (Alex Finch & Co) and from Vernon Hewett (AON) provided insightful responses.

Further useful comments were received from solicitors including Paul Worth at Eversheds and Richard Houseago at Greenwoods. John Andrew from LBC provided the forensic accountants viewpoint. I am grateful to Jonathan Samuelson at Harris Claims Group for considering my manuscript as a loss assessor.

In truth, I also owe a debt to the great number of individuals who have provided feedback in respect of a work book, that I have used for many years when running workshops, which formed the foundation of this book. Without their comments this work would not have been possible.

Damian Glynn
November 2005

Contents .... Page

Foreword

I am proud to sponsor a book written from a loss adjusting perspective, yet which is neither a claims nor loss adjusting textbook. BI Cover Issues has been written by one of our most experienced and talented business interruption adjusters. Damian is both a chartered loss adjuster and a chartered accountant and his role, over more than ten years, has been to contribute his expertise within our Specialist Adjusting Network, concentrating mainly on large and complex cases, requiring a multi-disciplinary response.

As loss adjusters we are expert in applying the policy wording to the specifics of the claim, whilst at the same time identifying and encouraging the policyholder to rehabilitate the enterprise that has been threatened by the incident which gave rise to our involvement. This provides us with an unrivalled experience at the sharp end and Damian has vividly and entertainingly illustrated his text with some of the scenarios that we have encountered.

Sadly, and far too frequently, we meet situations where either the scope or the value of the policy cover is inadequate. Owners of businesses that suffer significant damage already face serious challenges as they seek to rehabilitate their businesses in an increasingly competitive market place. If the cover is properly arranged, they stand a fighting chance of success. The purpose of this book is to use our practical experience to promote a better understanding of the issues that need to be addressed if the policyholder is to be provided with adequate and appropriate cover.

Our clients have a great track record in honouring the insurance promise and we in the loss adjusting community have a significant role to play in helping them do just that. It is our modest hope that this book will assist those responsible for designing and implementing appropriate insurance programmes.

Gerry Loughney
Chief Executive Officer
Cunningham Lindsey United Kingdom

1. Objective

This book has one main objective - to take the experience that claims provide and put it back into the process at the front end. This will allow insurance brokers and insurers to identify elements of business interruption insurance programmes meriting closer scrutiny before claims occur both for existing clients and with prospects. The aim is to be both pragmatic and accessible enough to be of use to purchasers of insurance in the corporate market, both risk managers and finance directors.

Loss adjusters are ideally placed to distil claims experiences that may have relevance to others in the future given that the claim is the point at which the policy stands or falls. In endeavouring to meet the objective, therefore, this book contains numerous practical examples that raise issues with a wider application.

It is necessary to summarise how the basic business interruption policy works to provide a context within which the claims experience can be presented. Likewise, it provides a starting point from which to consider the necessity for the various extensions to cover that can be purchased. More importantly, it ensures that the foundation stones of the business interruption policy (which can easily be taken for granted) are fully appreciated and considered when the policy is set-up.

There can be a tendency to shy away from providing too much technical explanation or detail, particularly in respect of business interruption to the client on the part of a broker, but it is the author's experience that technical detail is welcomed. Without a proper appreciation of the mechanics of the policy or an informed basis to compare different policies, it is hardly surprising that the purchase decision will often be based solely on price. Why pay more for something that is perceived to be an essentially identical (albeit repackaged) product?

No index has been produced for this book, which reflects the fact that it seeks to raise issues pre loss rather than providing specific assistance after a claim is made. Rather than being a reference to dip into in the hour of need, it is hoped that this book represents a self administered course. Computer based training without the computer, as it were.

2. The Core Cover

Consequential Losses

Historically, what is now known as business interruption cover was referred to as consequential loss (or loss of profits) insurance. Quite understandably, if you had a consequential loss insurance policy you might anticipate all consequences of fires, or of any other insured peril to be covered. However, there are numerous examples of elements of loss that would not be paid, including those losses which fall within the amount of an excess, those which are specifically excluded, or shortfalls due to material damage underinsurance.

There can be a tendency to perceive business interruption cover as a 'sweeper' policy paying for any loss that is not dealt with as part of the material damage claim.

Two specific examples of consequences of damage not covered by a standard policy may be helpful, wasted costs and (material damage) underinsurance.

Wasted Costs

An insured used packaging, the cost of which was categorised as part of Purchases in the profit and loss account and which was deducted from turnover in calculating Gross Profit, thereby uninsuring it. The packaging was purchased preprinted with customers' logos and was obviously specific to those particular contracts. The business suffered a fire and took various steps to mitigate the loss and, at first, the response from customers seemed very positive.

In the month after the fire, turnover to the main customer was maintained at the previous level, albeit at the expense of significant increased costs, pending the completion of physical repairs. Given that the customer appeared to be prepared to suffer minor inconvenience whilst permanent repairs were carried out, the insured business made its normal purchase of customer packaging which was typically bought in on a quarterly basis and in bulk.

Some two weeks after the purchase of the packaging, the customer advised that, whilst they accepted that the insured business had done all it could in the circumstances, the timing of the fire had caused very significant loss to them. They had, therefore, decided to move the business to another company who operated from several sites and did not present the same risk of a repeat occurrence ever happening. At that time the insured business still had a stock (at cost) of around £40,000 of packaging material with a customer's logo on that was not usable.

Nobody would dispute that the wasted costs incurred in purchasing this material represented a loss caused by the fire. The issue was whether this loss comprised a consequence that was actually covered by the policy. Given that the insured company had decided of its own volition to define Gross Profit for insurance purposes by deducting Purchases (defined as including packaging) from turnover, by definition it could not be paid as part of an insurance claim. The danger of presuming that significant costs will reduce proportionately with turnover is discussed in chapter 5.

Underinsurance

It is also the case that inadequacies in the material damage insurance cover can spill over into the business interruption claim. Consider the situation where an insured business purchased a significant piece of machinery second-hand for say £500,000 when its replacement cost might be £1,500,000. The Sum Insured will probably have been set with reference to the historic cost actually incurred rather than correctly reflecting the cost of replacement. If the funds are not available to replace the machine because the level of insurance under the material damage cover was set too low then it may well be that that machine will not be replaced, or may be replaced later.

If this is the case, then the business interruption policy would not respond to the additional losses which the delay in replacing the machine gave rise to. Technically, a decision not to replace plant for the reason set out above could constitute a failure on the part of the insured business to mitigate its loss. The common practice of insurers dealing with the claim but stripping out any increased element of loss caused by non replacement remains at the insurer's discretion and is not a right.

It is worth noting in making this observation, however, that underinsurance in respect of material damage cover does not necessarily have any impact at all on the business interruption. If the business is able to pull in finance from another source to make good any underinsurance difficulty then there will be no issue for the business interruption cover to consider.

That is not to say that a business might decide to take any particular expense, or part of the business, out of the remit of the insurance cover following a cost benefit analysis. Such a decision will be taken consciously and will not become a surprise at claims time. It will then neither be a shock to the insured business that no payment can be received in respect of the loss suffered, nor a shock to the broker if he is on the wrong end of a legal action where a perceived shortfall in the policy payment arises.

Two questions present themselves when considering the applicability of policy cover. Firstly, there is the question of whether a particular loss arises as a direct consequence of an insured incident. If the answer to that question is yes, then the second question presents itself: is this a consequence of Damage caused by an insured peril that is covered by the policy?

The Operative Clause

It is worthwhile taking a moment to consider the basis on which insurers will consider making any payment under a business interruption cover. Not only is the beginning of the policy a sensible starting point, but there are some basic issues that might be identified when its application to any particular business is considered. The standard All Risks business interruption wording suggested by the Association of British Insurers (ABI) is as follows:

'The insurer agrees (subject to the terms, definitions, exclusions, conditions of this policy) that if after payment of the first premium any building or other property used by the insured at the Premises for the purpose of the

Business be accidentally lost, destroyed or damaged during the period of insurance (or any subsequent period for which the insurer accepts a renewal premium) and in consequence the business carried on by the insured at the Premises be interrupted or interfered with then the insurer will pay to the insured in respect of each item in the Schedule the amount of loss resulting from such interruption or interference provided that:

1) *At the time of the happening of the loss destruction or damage there shall be in force an insurance covering the interest of the insured in the property at the Premises against such loss, destruction or damage and that*
   i) *payment should have been made or liability admitted therefor, or*
   ii) *payment would have been made or liability admitted therefor but for the operation of a proviso in such insurance excluding liability for losses below a specified amount.*

2) *The liability of the insurer under this policy shall not exceed*
   i) *in the whole the total sum insured or in respect of any item, its sum insured or any other limit of liability stated in the Schedule at the time of the loss, destruction or damage.*
   ii) *the sum insured (or limit) remaining after deduction for any other interruption or interference consequent upon loss, destruction or damage occurring during the same period of insurance unless the insurer shall have agreed to reinstate any such sum insured (or limit).”*

It follows from the above that four issues need to be quite clear:

a) The insured - is the insured entity properly and appropriately defined?

b) What are the Premises and has the Business carried out at each site (or elsewhere) been properly identified?

c) Has the Business been properly described? Any failure to identify key aspects of the business at inception can lead to difficulties should a claim be made.

d) Has the interest of the insured in relevant physical assets been insured against under a material damage cover and is it meaningful for this concept to be applied?

The issues of Damage and the Material Damage Proviso are separately considered below.

The Insured

Incorporation

Whilst it is an obvious statement that the insured person needs to be accurately identified, it is not uncommon to find policies issued in the name of a limited company when in fact the insured person is an unincorporated partnership, or vice versa. In the vast majority of cases this would have little relevance. An unincorporated partnership may have decided that the time had come to trade as a limited company, for example. The risk may be precisely as previously presented, but for the legal form that the business is conducted in. Notwithstanding that, there have been cases in the past where such a change in status has been viewed as a material fact by underwriters.

However, where, for example, part of a business operation may have been incorporated and part continued to run as a partnership confusion can arise as to what costs and income streams properly belong in each part of that operation. A policy may have been taken out covering one part of the business operation but not the other. Suppliers might be minded to continue invoicing the same legal entity that they always have, regardless of any legal change that the insured business may have decided to make. The legal form of the documentation might not reflect the economic substance intended by the insured business.

Whilst the production of the first set of accounts should provide a clear definition of the intention of what should lie where, claims have a nasty habit of occurring at the worst possible time and a claim could occur prior to that first set of accounts being prepared. The insured business might assume that gross profit losses would be covered, but which may have inadvertently been omitted from the scope of the policy.

Joint Ventures

The fundamental corporate structure of the core entity does not have to change for there to be an issue. There may be a business expansion involving a joint venture with another company. To keep the risks of that venture separate from the core entity, a further limited company may be set-up on a shared ownership basis. In a world of increasing collaboration, this arrangement is quite common.

Technically, depending on the share ownership of the new entity, such a joint venture business might not fall within the definition of a subsidiary were it to be the case that the insured business does not have dominant control. Issues such as voting rights of shares, or any preference that might be enjoyed by one party or another were the business to be wound up, or even the presence of directors' loans, could be relevant in determining this, but it would nevertheless remain an issue requiring consideration. Many policies are issued in the name of a holding company and/or subsidiary companies and a failure to explicitly include the joint venture operation could lead to a conclusion that it was not part of the insurance programme. Such a conclusion would be more likely where, for example, sums insured were not increased to reflect its existence before the claim occurs.

It is worth noting that it is not necessarily a good idea for all participants in a joint venture to be formally acknowledged in the policy. Banks, for example, have no direct interest in the success of a venture. An overly long list of participants may result in delay in settling a claim.

Corporate Groups

Another example of how a group structure can cause difficulties is when the policy subsists in the name of a business that perhaps historically was the holding company. Over time the group structure may have become more complex and that holding company may have become one of a number of operating subsidiaries of another entity. If the policy still remains in the name of what is now a subsidiary company then technically businesses higher up the group hierarchy, or fellow subsidiaries of such businesses would have no cover.

Any misunderstandings might be cleared-up were it to be the case that a proper premium overall has been paid and that despite the terminology of the schedule, the insurers appreciated what they were underwriting. However, they might not, and delay could occur whilst the matter is clarified (as has been the case where this complication has arisen in the past). Where underinsurance applies and there is a lack of clarity as to which businesses are covered by the policy, the time taken to resolve the matter can be significant and not necessarily resolved to the preference of the insured business.

Undisclosed Agency

It is worth noting that nobody is at liberty to set-up an insurance cover as undisclosed agent for another. There have been cases in the past where the insured person identified on the schedule is little more than a participant in a business network representing a whole range of interests. If insurers were unaware of this and did not have the opportunity to consider the risks presented by what in effect would be a collection of insured persons rather than just the one initially presented, then an adverse response could be provided at claims time.

This can happen where one member of an extended family running a range of businesses is understood by insurers to be the insured person without any mention of anybody else.

Another parallel would be a tenant arranging buildings insurance when they only occupy part of the demised premises. The tenant would only have an insurable interest for those parts of the building that they occupy and for the common areas, but not for those parts of the premises occupied by other tenants. Assuming that the landlord has forgotten to insure his buildings at all (and this happens), the tenant would be faced with the difficulty of trying to negotiate reconstruction of a very much reduced footprint (even assuming landlord co-operation). The tenant might feel aggrieved if he has been paying a premium in respect of the whole building only to find that a lack of insurable interest allows him to claim in respect of only part of it.

The Ruling Mind

Of course, a limited company is a separate legal entity, but its ruling mind comprises the board of directors. Most proposal forms will ask questions about the directors to allow insurers to consider all aspects of the risk, including moral risk, details of any criminal past on the part of a director or bankruptcy or insolvency that they may have historically been involved in. It is worth observing that, whilst the Rehabilitation of Offenders Act provides a framework for historic criminal convictions not to be disclosed once they have lapsed (the time period prior to lapsing varies according to the severity of the crime, the most heinous crimes never lapsing), there is no such closure period for bankruptcy/insolvency which, of course, is not a criminal act.

There have been a number of cases of misunderstanding where historic bankruptcies have not been disclosed and are only identified on enquiry when a claim is made.

The disclosure issues for directors of companies or principals of unincorporated businesses are always worth reviewing on a regular basis.

Shadow Directors
Sometimes difficulty is experienced not in dealing with undisclosed issues in respect of those named as directors, but rather in identifying other individuals who are not listed as statutory directors but who nevertheless actually run the business. An individual may adopt a very modest title but Companies Act 1985 asserts that the term 'Director' *"includes any person occupying the position of director, by whatever name called"* (Section 741). The legislation refers to such an individual as a 'shadow director' who is essentially an individual in accordance with whose instruction the board tends to act.

This might be deliberately arranged for unsatisfactory reasons. An individual may historically have been disqualified from acting as a director or they may have a criminal past. In the latter regard, it is not uncommon to deal with claims where an individual held out to insurers as the sole director of a business turns out to be the mother, for example, of the individual actually running the operation. She may confirm, when formally interviewed, that she has nothing to do with the business at all and never even visits the premises.

The objective of arranging matters this way may be to avoid having to disclose unsavoury answers to questions raised in respect of directors (albeit it is accepted that need not be the case). The plan would fail, as the Companies Act provisions relating to shadow directors would bring the undisclosed individual actually running the business within the remit of the questions on the proposal form relating to directors. An undisclosed moral risk of a serious nature could, therefore, lead to voidance of the policy and non-payment of the claim.

In some cases, the person actually running the business does not appear either as a director or a shareholder for reasons that may not be entirely clear. On one occasion, a carpet importer was clearly the only person of any significance in his business, and was the person that dealt with both customers and suppliers. The only director and apparent shareholder of the business was his secretary. The man running the business was quite evasive initially as to why the business had been arranged in this way, and, against the backdrop of an arson having taken place, it was something that needed to be properly understood. Ultimately, it was established that the man had been through a messy divorce and perceived that he had been very harshly treated in respect of the division of assets between himself and his previous wife. To prevent any further complication he moved to England and had decided to have as few assets in his own name as possible to prevent a recurrence.

Insurers subsequently agreed to deal with the claim notwithstanding the convoluted arrangements surrounding the business although the confirmation of indemnity was delayed by around three months whilst investigation was ongoing. Had that insured person properly explained the situation to his insurance broker at inception or even promptly co-operated with loss adjusters following the claim, then such a delay could have been avoided.

The Business

Only the **business named**, undertaking the **activities described**, at the **Premises** listed in the policy is going to be recompensed should a claim be made.

Complementary Businesses
There are many complementary activities that insured businesses can enter into alongside their core activity, which they may have forgotten to mention when incepting the policy. A firm of chartered accountants may engage in insolvency work, for example, but may have forgotten to advise their insurers about this.

Insolvency work carries different risks and exposure from core audit work and insurers might like to have considered the same in advance of a claim. A loss of utilities for a few days would be unlikely to give rise to a loss of audit fee income over a twelve-month Maximum Indemnity Period for example, but the non-availability of an insolvency practitioner if a decision suddenly has to be made by a bank with regards to the appointment of such an individual could give rise to a discrete business interruption loss.

Rental Income
More businesses are becoming small-time landlords, seeking to make best use of their fixed cost base. Renting out a building or perhaps part of a building (as a concession in a retail environment) will produce rental income as distinct from the Gross Profit of the business operation forming the core activity. There will be a need to ensure that this element of business is notified to insurers.

It is not uncommon for the pension fund of a limited company to own the buildings from which the business itself operates. Frequently, the pension fund is insured under one policy and the limited company under another. This might be represented in simple form as follows:

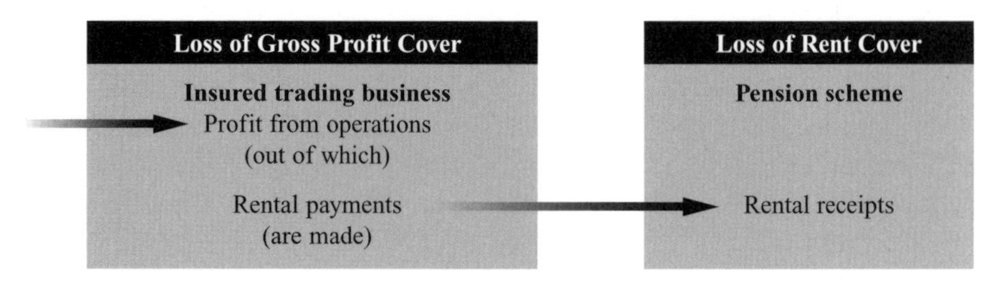

The limited company earns gross profit, part of which is used to pay the rent. In other words, the gross profit includes the rent expense, assuming that this is not specifically uninsured. If the pension scheme also has a policy relating to the loss of rent, there may be double counting. If the shareholders in the limited company are also amongst the main beneficiaries of the pension scheme, such double counting might not be desirable.

Assuming that there is no rent cessation clause, the limited company could elect to continue paying rent after the operation of an insured peril, funded by the interim payments received from insurers (assuming that policy conditions and warranties are complied with). The rental income enjoyed by the pension scheme would not be at risk.

On the other hand, inadvertent omission of cover is also a danger. If the lease on the Premises has a rent cessation clause, the pension scheme will need Loss of Rent cover.

If the pension fund is named as a joint insured entity in the policy of the limited company then the danger of omission or of double counting does not arise.

The case of the pension fund is offered as a corollary to the need to specifically include rental income in most other situations and clearly would not be appropriate where participants in the pension fund are not coterminous with the participants in the operational core activity to any significant degree.

New Operations

It might be the case that a new business development could constitute an activity sufficiently different from the main business to require formal expansion of the description of the business on the schedule. This would be relevant to a business previously engaged in warehousing exploring the operation of retail units (as some of the large cash and carry warehouses have done), or considering an expansion from warehousing to haulage (or vice versa). Alternatively, a business expanding from software design to hardware sales would be significantly altering the profile of its risk.

Not all businesses expand in a complementary and synergistic manner - an entrepreneurial business may identify an opportunity to purchase a company at a very modest price in an unfamiliar industry sector. It is not uncommon to deal with a group of businesses where one or more subsidiaries bear no relationship to the others. In one case, one subsidiary company sold life jackets whereas the other group businesses were involved in powder coating, anodising and electroplating for a wide range of customers.

Of course, there are also bizarre examples of a change in direction for an insured company. Consider the following:

A business reconditioned second-hand sewing machines, as far as the insurers were aware. This business suffered the theft of a desktop computer and submitted a business interruption claim in excess of £750,000. Upon enquiry it became apparent that the loss had arisen because a tender document to be issued the morning after the theft, which had been saved on the hard disk of the stolen computer, had been lost (there was no separate backup of the data on another machine and no Warranty in the policy requiring the same). The tender, however, had nothing to do with sewing machines. A contact overseas had brought to the insured business' attention an opportunity to provide a tender for the supply of military small arms to a foreign government.

The contact was, in fact, the person receiving all of the tenders in that government and advised that they would discreetly open all other tenders ten minutes before the deadline. They would then telephone the insured business so that a marginally lower tender figure could be inserted in the pre-prepared document and immediately e-mailed. The actual arrangement of the arms supply would be dealt with by the contact but the insured business would enjoy a significant level of profit participation in return for its assistance. The theft of the computer prevented the issue of the tender and deprived the insured of the opportunity to submit the tender document at the last moment.

Setting aside the legal and moral issues, the supply of armaments to foreign governments did not comprise part of the business presented to insurers and the claim was declined. As might be expected the insurers declined to renew at the end of the policy period which, in fact, occurred very shortly after the incident date.

Whilst the above true example may be extreme, it illustrates the point.

Trading Unlawfully

The business which is presented to insurers should be run in accordance with the law. The case of *Roger Owen James - v- CGU (2001)* concerned a business that was in dispute with Customs and Excise and the Revenue on a number of counts. The disputes were not disclosed to insurers. In essence, the judge confirmed the insurer's position that this was a moral issue that should have been disclosed to underwriters to allow them to consider all aspects of the risk. (Interestingly, it was confirmed that materiality, in terms of non disclosure, referred to the relevance of issues to the prudent underwriter, not the significance of those issues to the insuring businessman.)

On another occasion, this time not involving litigation, a claim for around £3,500,000 (business interruption) was submitted, where the circumstances giving rise to the claim were not under suspicion but it became clear that the business was being conducted fraudulently. Adult clothing was being described as childrens' clothing to avoid payment of VAT to Customs and Excise. The policy was avoided ab initio on the basis of non disclosure. This was not seriously contested by the claimant company. There have been other instances where businesses generated significant levels of turnover, very significantly higher than the VAT threshold, without paying any VAT. This could constitute fraudulent trading depending on the business' VAT status.

For clarification, the VAT position can be summarised as follows:

VAT Status	Charge VAT on sales	Recover VAT on purchases	Include VAT on Material Damage Sums Insured
Standard Rated	Yes	Yes	No
Zero Rated	No	Yes	No
Exempt	No	No	Yes

(The above table ignores composite rate tax payers. Additionally, the position of landlords who may opt to tax particular properties may require a different approach to setting material damage sums insured for some properties compared to others.)

A failure to deduct PAYE from staff wages or to account for income tax, for example, is as much a concern as non-payment of VAT.

It should be stressed that the comments being made relate to a deliberate intent to flout the law rather than a delay in payment, in respect of which the law provides sanctions in the form of fines, penalties, and the levying of interest. VAT fraud merely happens to be more apparent for two reasons. Firstly, VAT returns are generally requested by loss adjusters to confirm turnover figures in claims, whereas PAYE details, by way of contrast, may not be fundamental. Secondly, VAT returns are (usually) submitted within one month after the end of the quarter to which they relate. A deliberate intent to trade fraudulently is apparent over a relatively short time period - an example presents itself every three months.

Books and Records
Assuming that a valid business has been properly presented to insurers, the cover can only relate to what goes through the books. This relates to businesses deliberately leaving monies out of their official records. A claim from a landlady in Skegness was excellently presented with contact details of a huge throng of people who had knocked on her door hoping to secure accommodation. They had to be turned away because of an escape of water in part of a building at the rear. Contact details were provided to loss adjusters for each of the callers and adjusters were encouraged to contact them to verify their details.

Unfortunately, when the income that it was claimed had been lost was added to that actually retained, total revenue many multiples higher than had ever been recorded in the books presented itself. This would have suggested a very significant shortfall in the Estimated Gross Profit provided to insurers. On that particular occasion the insurers dealt with the claim, but limited any payment to that part of the business reflected in the books. Another insurer may have taken a different stance and decided that the (undisclosed) moral risk suggested by the way the business was conducted, supported policy voidance.

Dishonesty is not the only issue to consider here. In the case of hotels, for example, tipping income for staff may be significant. In some establishments tips are retained by the employer. In others tips are shared between the employer and staff. In other cases the staff enjoy them outright. In the latter case, the monies may not be shown as income within the business' books, being retained directly by the staff. The employer may not even know the amounts involved where these are paid in cash. An agreement may have been reached with the HM Revenue & Customs in respect of tax due on notional levels of tips but this again may be a private matter which the employer knows nothing about.

After a fire, even if the employer continues to pay the staff wages pending reinstatement, tipping income, which may not be part of the insured business for the reason set out above, may be significantly depleted and staff may find that they have to seek employment elsewhere. When the damage is repaired the business will still be hampered by the absence of staff. Where these are relatively unskilled and replaceable that may not be an issue, but an experienced maître d' is an individual that the insured business will wish to retain. Potentially, additional payments to staff might be entertained as increased costs but this is not necessarily so and is an example of an income stream dependent upon the business that might not be reflected in the books but in respect of which some form of insurance arrangement might be desirable.

The Premises

The operative clause provides cover for losses incurred by the business at the Premises. The term Premises has a capital letter which signifies that the term will be clarified in the definition section. Unfortunately, Premises is invariably defined as 'the Premises in the schedule' rather than defining which physical assets at the address identified falls within the cover. There are three general issues to consider under the heading 'Premises', being the scope of the cover, the trade conducted at the Premises, and the basis of tenure.

Scope of Cover

A fire occurred in a building on a secure site, set back from the public highway some considerable distance. A fairly long roadway had to be navigated prior to reaching the site proper and there were numerous hard standings on the site, pieces of plant in the open providing services as well as the buildings themselves. At face value the whole site comprised the Premises and it was a matter for insurers to consider whether the roadways and the general apparatus on-site were all brought within the cover.

Were it to be the case that they should be, then the material damage sum insured would be very significantly understated and a large shortfall would have been experienced in respect of the fire at the damaged building. Had that been the case, then the European parent company may have decided that it was not prepared to fund the uninsured investment required to repair the Damage, resulting in potential closure of the site and ensuing complication in settling the business interruption claim.

Following further investigation and discussion, the insured business was able to demonstrate that there had been previous incidents affecting the roadway which had not resulted in claims under the insurance policy. (Roads are, it is acknowledged, specifically excluded from some material damage wordings.) This was accepted as evidence that it was not the intention, at least on the part of the insured, for such features to form part of the cover and supported the contention that they should be omitted from the calculation of the value at risk. Consequently, the sum insured was adequate and the claim dealt with satisfactorily.

Many businesses have racking in the yard on which stock is stored, sometimes of a hazardous nature, and it is not always clear whether the intention is to insure the Premises in terms of the building only and the contents thereof or the demised Premises in surveying terms (i.e. the curtillage at the postal address).

The above comments are not intended to suggest that the stock stored in the open would generally be insured - insurer's specific agreement to include it would be necessary. Mere clarification of the definition of Premises would be insufficient.

Significant business interruption claims have arisen following damage outside the building but within the postal address and such incidents can potentially fall between stools as far as cover is concerned. They may not be intended to fall within the cover of the Premises (were this to be interpreted as the buildings only) and Damage to them might not satisfy the Material Damage Proviso. However, neither would Damage to assets outside a building be dealt with through the various extensions to the core policies such as denial of access since it would not have occurred off site. Given the lack of detail and the definition of Premises in the policy, in the case of any doubt pre claim clarification will assist.

The term Premises can have a very wide application. Premises embraces, for example, inspection pits set into pavements giving access to underground utilities.

Consider the following:

> *A vehicle drove into a wall along a cliffside coastal road, sending debris down the hillside, some of which caused Damage to a café further down the slope. The impact had damaged an advertisement hoarding belonging to the café as well as structurally damaging the wall and its support such that the local authority forbade the café to open for business until repair works had been carried out. The danger of further debris falling until that point remained significant.*
>
> *Lacking any extensions to the basic business interruption cover, the café submitted a claim on the basis that the Damage occurred at the Premises in the sense that the cliff overhung the footprint of the demised café Premises below the point where the impact occurred. This claim raised the issue of whether the airspace above a site comprised part of the Premises, and, if so, to what height.*

The example is unusual, but illustrates the fact that apparently simple issues, such as identification of the Premises, may not be straightforward to resolve. Had the insured business identified the importance of the advertising hoarding pre claim, underwriters might have been prepared to bring it (and Damage to it) within the cover. It is worth noting that the café example, whilst unusual, is not unique. Permanent advertising hoardings at sports grounds illustrating retailers' and manufacturers' products have been added to the list of Premises on policy schedules in the past.

Trade at the Premises

There is the concern from a business interruption perspective that focusing the cover on the Premises may not embrace all of the activities of the insured business. Consider the sale of ice cream by a business operating ice cream vans as well as selling from site.

Following Damage at the defined Premises there may be an inability to make the product and to achieve any turnover. On one occasion, significant discussion ensued as to whether that element of turnover representing sales from vans on the road constituted the business at the Premises. Insurers accepted that on balance they were aware that some of the turnover was achieved from the vans, albeit this was still dependent on production at the defined Premises and the claim was paid.

The issue here was that the Damage at the defined Premises was what gave rise to the claim rather than Damage to a van. The vans could be replaced - the business interruption exposure remained focused on the site. (Lost turnover due to Damage to a van away from the Premises would not be covered under a standard business interruption policy.)

This is to be contrasted with the situation where sales are primarily achieved off site, for example, via salesmen selling jewellery or other valuables on the basis of samples carried with them. In that situation, an event which deprives the salesman of his samples (theft whilst he is on the road, for example) could result in very significant business interruption losses. The salesman securing custom from samples is the effective equivalent of the shop window. Particularly in the case of jewellery, the time taken to remanufacture bespoke samples might be significant. (A transit extension to the cover might be of assistance in such cases.)

A parallel situation occurs where a business provides a service at customer sites. This is a very common situation in the construction industry, for consultants, be they management, IT, or other, engineers or the providers of a wide range of professional services. The Premises defined in the policy provide the base location and administrative support, but the turnover is achieved off site. Business interruption cover that is only available after Damage occurs at the Premises might be insufficient. Either the insured business needs to appreciate any limitation in cover pre loss, or further discussion with insurers is required to establish what further cover may be available, if this is considered desirable.

The business interruption risk might be lessened (spread) if services are provided at a multitude of customer sites. Whilst an incident at any one customer location might produce some loss of profit, it would be most unlikely for many customer sites to be affected at the same time and the amount involved in any particular incident may, therefore, be modest.

This issue is not only relevant to the core Gross Profit cover, it might also suggest the need for a customers' extension. The standard policy wording would not deal with claims arising at customers' Premises unless such a customers' extension had been purchased, albeit some wordings provide cover by default, allowing claims of up to 10% of the Sum Insured in respect of incidents at customers' sites even without a specific request for such cover. The Premium cost of such an extension may be unattractive if there is a low risk of a significant claim.

For businesses involved in long-term contracts with customers and long-term commissioning projects there may be a significant exposure flowing from Damage at a particular location and there will be a need to expand the basic cover accordingly. This might be achieved through a contract works policy or under a customers extension as discussed in chapter 3.

Any business that generates significant levels of business on the basis of activities away from the Premises will benefit from more detailed consideration of the applicability of the core policy.

Tenure

Being a tenant as opposed to a freeholder in itself increases the business interruption risk.

A tenant is likely to have little control over the speed of building repairs following the occurrence of an insured event and consequently is unable to control a mitigation strategy to minimise a business interruption claim in the way that would be possible if the building was owned.

Many landlords and their loss adjusters will be receptive to the suggestion that the tenant's business interruption insurers fund acceleration of repair works following Insured Damage, such that reoccupation of the damaged building and resumption of production can occur at the earliest possible time. Not only will the landlord want to be seen to be helping his tenant to the extent that he is able (assuming that the tenant is desirable), but the landlord's loss adjusters will also be mindful that his Loss of Rent claim is also dependent on the time scale involved. Some form of contribution from the landlord's own business interruption insurer in recognition of this is normal.

The idea that the landlord will not object to acceleration seems very logical but there have been claims where, almost inexplicably, there has been a reluctance to provide such co-operation. If the landlord is particularly wealthy with a large portfolio he may be less reliant on the income stream from the damaged Premises than the tenant is on the profit he generates there. The landlord may not wish to be hurried in replacing an asset on which he will rely in the long-term merely to placate a tenant with whom there may be a relationship in the short-term.

The landlord, in common with the tenant, may take the opportunity that the insured incident presents to review his business strategy and question whether reinstatement on the same basis or even on the same site is desirable. There would be no objection from the landlord's insurer were he to decide to rebuild elsewhere.

To some extent any lease in place would likely require the landlord to reinstate. However, this would not deny the landlord a reasonable opportunity to consider the precise form of such reinstatement. In practice it would be difficult to demonstrate that there has been a fundamental failure on the part of the landlord to fulfil his lease obligations merely because he has not moved as rapidly as the tenant would like.

An owner occupier may be able to cut corners to some extent, through informal discussion with the relevant planning authority. However, the landlord may have no particular imperative to do the same and it would be difficult to criticise a landlord for merely allowing the local authority to exercise its, often slow moving, function in the normal course of events. The tenant's indemnity period may be longer as a consequence. A tenant may never have considered asking the landlord to confirm what amount the relevant building has been insured for, and it must be a mere presumption that the amount selected by the landlord is adequate. Shortfalls due to the omission of an allowance for professional fees or debris removal cover are not uncommon. Many policies incorporate underinsurance provisions that only reduce a claim when a sum insured is less than 85% of what it ought to be (the value at risk), thereby allowing some margin of error in favour of the insured person.

On numerous occasions in the past the landlord's sum insured has been significantly understated. Where the landlord subsequently experiences a shortfall of funds with regards his claim, this has inevitably impacted upon the replacement timetable resulting in increased business interruption losses, for both landlord and tenant.

The situation can be even worse for a landlord with a wide portfolio. It is not unknown for a particular address to be omitted entirely from a schedule of Premises featuring many locations such that there is no insurance cover available for the landlord at all following the damage. If underinsurance was likely to give rise to some form of delay, a failure to insure at all on the part of the landlord could vastly exacerbate the chronology involved to the extent that the tenant might need to give serious consideration to a permanent relocation.

Moving to another address is never an easy matter, but this can be critical if a presence on the high street, for example, is vital as may be the case for a retailer. High street furniture stores in urban clusters around major cities will invariably wither if not located on an arterial route.

Specialist locations are likewise vulnerable. Following a fire at a "gentlemens' club", it was considered impractical to try and relocate temporarily even for a year. It was concluded that the patrons might take a sufficiently long time to identify the new address that turnover would not pickup to reasonable levels prior to the expiry of the Maximum Indemnity Period.

There is no simple solution, but there are issues arising merely by virtue of a tenancy existing in so far as the length of the period that the business interruption cover should be insured for.

As a side note, there is nothing to stop a tenant, from a risk management point of view, discussing with a landlord a protocol for the reinstatement of damage prior to it occurring. For modest claims of, say, up to £25,000, the landlord may be happy for a tenant to immediately effect repairs, assuming that these are undertaken on a like for like basis. The landlord can subsequently identify what he believes to be that proportion of the repair costs that he would have incurred had the matter been tendered or given to his preferred supplier. The balance might be claimed by the tenant as an increased cost under his business interruption policy.

There may be complications with regards to VAT if such protocols are established, particularly if the landlord is not VAT registered but the tenant is. In such a situation, the tenant's cost recharge to the landlord would need to have VAT added to it.

Insurers would need to be brought into discussion to approve such a plan before it commenced and the acceptability of such a scheme to the landlord would in large part depend upon his relationship and trust in the tenant and the latter's financial solvency.

Damage and the Material Damage Proviso

It is not possible to obtain business interruption cover in respect of fire, flood, theft or any other peril.

What can be purchased is business interruption cover flowing from Damage caused by an insured peril, or in the case of an All Risks policy from an external cause not otherwise excluded.

Whilst the distinction may appear to be semantic, it brings clarity to numerous difficult areas. The exacerbation of a business interruption claim due to severe material damage underinsurance would introduce an element of loss not flowing solely and directly from Damage, for example. It would at least partly be caused by an error in setting the relevant sums insured.

Damage is generally a defined term but the definition rarely adds anything substantive, invariably referring to 'damage or loss'.

The Operative Clause has been previously discussed. It will be clear from that there is a requirement for there to be in force an insurance covering the interest of the insured in the property that has been damaged, and for a payment to have been made in respect of that except for the operation of an excess. This is known as the Material Damage Proviso. The proviso is not a qualified term - either it is satisfied or it is not. Fire damage (assuming actual ignition) amounting to 1p will satisfy the proviso just as much as a fire causing damage requiring £1,000,000 of repairs.

However, merely satisfying the material damage proviso does not mean that the claimed business interruption loss will be covered. The business interruption losses that are being claimed still have to flow from the Damage (unlikely in the example offered where repairs cost only 1p). The following may help to clarify the situation:

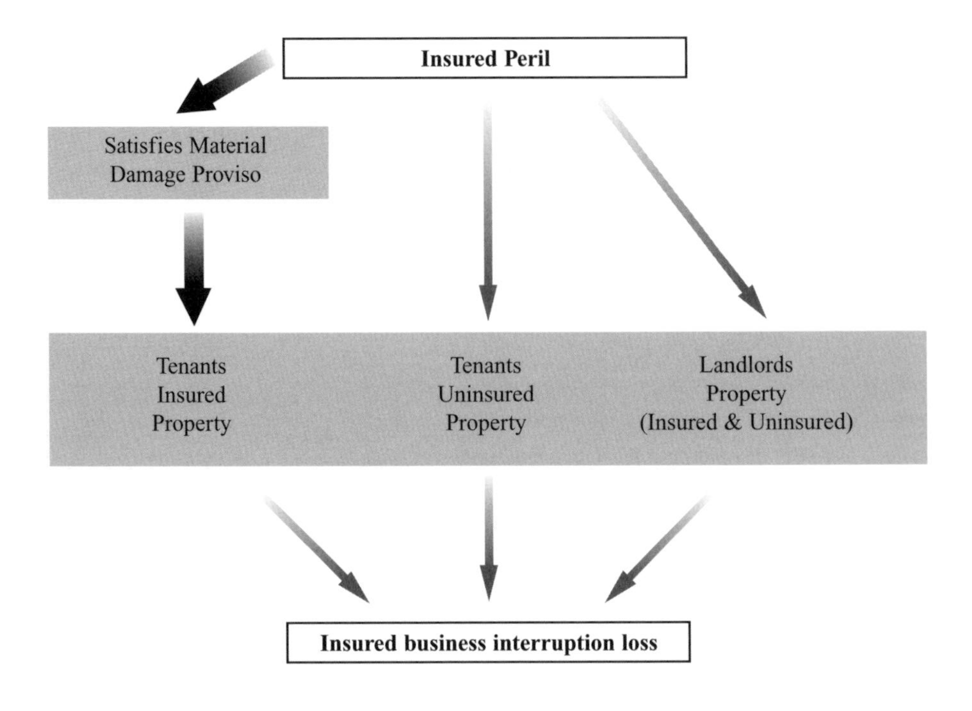

In the above scenario, the insured person is a tenant in a retail unit and an escape of water has damaged carpets and fixtures that he has installed as well as the underlying concrete floor and structure owned by the landlord. The damage to the carpets and fixtures, the tenant's insured property, (denoted by the bold arrow) would satisfy the Material Damage Proviso. However, the business interruption cover does not restrict the business interruption loss to a loss of profit solely deriving from that aspect of Damage that satisfied the proviso.

The tenant's business interruption policy would also deal with losses arising from Damage caused by the insured peril to property in a wider sense. The carpet could not be laid until the landlord's floor had dried out and repaired, and an interruption period of say one month or two might arise. The tenant's business interruption cover would not be restricted to the two to three working days that it might otherwise take to simply lay a new carpet. The losses flowing from the (damaged) landlords property which the tenant uses for his business (which may or may not be insured), would also be covered.

There is no requirement for the tenant to have legal ownership of the assets which suffer Damage. Using those assets for the purpose of the business provides an insurable interest and these are brought within the cover, including assets that are leased (whether a finance or operating lease).

Assets which may be loaned by a customer, supplier or joint venture partner are again relevant. There may be no material damage insurance in respect of those but the business interruption loss that derives therefrom caused by the operation of an insured peril where this has also damaged other property insured by the business is covered.

Satisfaction of the proviso does not restrict business interruption losses to merely those that derive directly from Damage to the assets that satisfy the proviso itself. However, the Damage must still be the proximate cause of loss.

Consider two sandwich shops in an urban centre suffering bomb damage. The first sandwich shop may suffer a hairline crack as a result of the explosion in the bottom corner of the front window, whereas the second sandwich shop may be fortunate enough to suffer no damage. For many months thereafter the turnover of both shops is likely to be depressed if neighbouring office units have suffered direct damage, office workers no longer being in the vicinity to eat the sandwiches on sale. Whilst one shop has satisfied the Material Damage Proviso and the other has not, the business interruption losses do not predominantly derive from the Damage that the first shop has suffered. The business interruption loss arising from the absence of customers would accrue regardless of the presence of the crack or not and would not therefore be recoverable under the policy.

Another example concerned a securities trading firm losing its telephone systems after storm damage. Business interruption losses arose. On enquiry, the main trading partners were found to have suffered similar problems. Even if the firm's telephone systems had been undamaged, it would not have been able to contact the customers in the immediate aftermath. The Damage suffered did not cause a loss over and above that arising from the non-availability of customers.

Alternatively, consider a coach and bus hire company which suffers a fire at its Premises overnight, damaging buildings, contents, and vehicles. Typically, one policy will cover the buildings, contents, and business interruption, and another policy will deal with the motor fleet risk. The business interruption cover will respond to the reduction in turnover arising from the Damage to the vehicles as well as to the buildings/contents despite such Damage being insured elsewhere (or even insured at all). That situation of course contrasts with Damage to the vehicles away from the Premises, which would not satisfy the Material Damage Proviso (unless the policy was suitably extended).

It should be noted that Damage by definition excludes the operation of equipment as intended. The issue of power surges blowing fuses regularly presents itself. A blown fuse is not a damaged fuse. It has operated as planned and the Material Damage Proviso will not be satisfied in that case. (Any subsequent fire Damage would be covered.)

There are few legal cases relating directly to business interruption, but there was a case that came before the courts directly dealing with the issue of the Material Damage Proviso, *Glengate - KG Properties Ltd -v- Norwich Union Fire Insurance Society Ltd and Others (1995).*

In this case, Glengate, a firm of developers, were redeveloping a department store in Oxford Street, central London, and therein were some drawings purchased by Glengate from the former owner's architects and around £100,000 of additional drawings prepared on-site by Glengate's design team. Glengate also insured the building itself. A policy covering the future rental income was taken out. A fire occurred and the material damage claim (including damage to the building) was accepted.

The Material Damage Proviso was satisfied and the business interruption loss that arose through delayed completion of the development because of the damage to the drawings was also covered. Those drawings themselves were not insured by Glengate but suffered damage from the same peril that had satisfied the Material Damage Proviso by virtue of it damaging the building.

In accordance with the diagram set out previously, this case confirms that the business interruption losses flowing from damage to uninsured property should be dealt with, assuming that the proviso has in the first instance been satisfied.

As an aside, the judge also confirmed that the proviso is not qualitative - underinsurance in terms of the architect's drawings would not have debarred recovery under the business interruption cover. As with any case, there were issues arising that were dealt with on the merits of the particular case in question.

Importantly, the Glengate case did differentiate between a broad insurable interest and a more narrow personal interest. An example of the former would be a tenant's interest in a building that he occupies. Despite having a broad insurable interest, the tenant would often not effect an insurance, leaving that instead for the landlord to deal with. The tenant would have the more narrow insurable interest in his own plant and machinery. A failure on the tenant's part to insure the building would not breach the Material Damage Proviso. However, a failure to effect an insurance where there is a narrower interest could constitute a breach. (Item 1 of the Operative Clause set out on page 14 specifies the requirement for insurance to be in force where there is (the narrower personal) insurable interest.) Whilst Glengate had a general insurable interest in the architect's drawings, it was not sufficiently narrow to require Glengate to have insured them. There was, therefore, no breach of the Material Damage Proviso.

Whilst not a common practice, insurers may agree to waive the Material Damage Proviso in particular circumstances - professional service companies selling knowledge rather than generating profit from tangible assets might find it difficult to ever satisfy the Proviso and to then be able to make a business interruption claim.

The relevance of discussing the detail of the Material Damage Proviso is twofold.

Firstly, it explains the interface between material damage and business interruption insurance and, partly as a result of the tangible nature of the former, it may be more readily appreciated as an initial point of reference.

Secondly, consideration of the Proviso helps to identify those businesses who have income streams at risk irrespective of material damage. An extreme example would be a (hobby) tutor teaching children how to dance in a village hall. Such an individual would not have assets that might be damaged and, therefore, the Material Damage Proviso might never be satisfied. Tenants in public houses might not own any assets or have material damage insurance but still have profits at risk. Some businesses generate profit on the basis of intellectual know-how rather than assets. All of these require careful review in the same way as businesses that generate income streams away from the Premises.

Different policy wordings give rise to a range of possible responses when an insured incident occurs. Discussion of the intention and scope of the cover with insurers will avoid misunderstandings.

The Mechanics of Cover

It was earlier affirmed that this book does not set out to be a manual of how business interruption losses should be calculated in detail nor of the technical approach that might be taken in any particular case to investigate the claim and agree quantum.

Notwithstanding that, it is necessary to explain in general terms how the business interruption loss will be calculated were there to be a claim so that the component parts can be considered in detail in advance to avoid misunderstandings arising.

Summary of cover

The Association of British Insurers (ABI) standard wording in respect of business interruption cover is as follows:

> *"The insurance under Item No.1 (Gross Profit) is limited to Loss of Gross Profit due to a) Reduction in Turnover and b) Increase in Cost of Working and the amount payable as indemnity there under shall be:*
>
> *a) in respect of Reduction in Turnover the sum produced by applying the Rate of Gross Profit to the amount by which the Turnover during the Indemnity Period shall fall short of the Standard Turnover in consequence of the Incident*
>
> *b) in respect of Increase in Cost of Working, the additional expenditure (subject to the provisions of the Uninsured Standing Charges Clause) necessarily and reasonably incurred for the sole purpose of avoiding or diminishing the reduction in Turnover which but for that expenditure would have taken place during the Indemnity Period in consequence of the Incident, but not exceeding the sum produced by applying the Rate of Gross Profit to the amount of the reduction thereby avoided*

less any sum saved during the indemnity period in respect of such of the charges and expenses of the Business payable out of Gross Profit as may cease or be reduced as a consequent of the Incident."

Standard definitions include the following:

"Turnover: The money paid or payable to the insured for goods sold and delivered and for services rendered in course of the Business at the Premises."

"Indemnity Period: The period beginning with the occurrence of the Incident and ending not later than the Maximum Indemnity Period thereafter during which the results of the Business shall be affected in consequence thereof."

"Gross Profit: The amount by which:

i) the sum of the amount of the Turnover and the amounts of the closing stock and work in progress shall exceed
ii) the sum of the amounts of the opening stock and work in progress and the amount of the Uninsured Working Expenses.

***Note**: The amount of the opening and closing stocks and work in progress shall be arrived at in accordance with the insured's normal accountancy methods, due provision being made for depreciation."*

The policy provides for three elements of a business interruption loss calculation. These comprise a **Loss of Gross Profit** (consequent upon a reduction in Turnover), **Increased Costs of Working** and **Savings**.

Loss of Gross Profit

The impact of an incident upon a business is measured in terms of a decline in turnover. The turnover generated in those months in the previous year corresponding with the period affected by the insured incident is referred to as the Standard Turnover. This is then adjusted for any necessary trend such that it then represents the turnover that would have been anticipated but for the insured event. This is referred to as the Adjusted Standard Turnover.

Actual turnover generated is deducted from the Adjusted Standard Turnover to calculate the Reduction in Turnover.

The Rate of Gross Profit as defined in the policy, (and discussed more fully below) is then applied to the Reduction in Turnover. It is not necessary to compare levels of gross profit on a month by month basis pre and post incident - the policy establishes the quantum of the loss initially on the turnover line. This avoids the complication that consideration and quantification of the greater number of variables that impact on gross profit would entail. The financial variation in the turnover can be more easily related directly back to the Damage.

Importantly, this item of cover relates to a Loss of Gross Profit consequent upon a Reduction in Turnover and not necessarily any Loss of Gross Profit from any other cause.

Turnover

The definition of turnover relates to the operation of the business at the Premises. Were turnover to be derived to any significant degree off site then clarification of this definition might be advisable. Businesses with long-term contracts may need to consider the term 'turnover' with some degree of care. An interim stage payment may have been received part way through a contract following which a catastrophic loss may be suffered which renders completion of the overall contract to be impractical. A return of the monies received to date may in certain circumstances be required. Such a repayment of funds would not constitute a loss of the turnover that would be reflected in the books but for the incident - the turnover, in accordance with accounting standards, may have been reflected in the accounts of a prior period. A loss which is a consequence of the incident, but not covered by the policy, might arise.

The definition of turnover for businesses earning a commission on the sale of tickets, for example, can also benefit from consideration and clarification. It is not uncommon for such a business to insure only the margin that it earns on sales in its business interruption policy. However, the revenue in the financial accounts may include gross receipts, with the cost of buying the tickets for resale shown within cost of sales.

For a Gross Profit cover, the net position should, in principle, be the same whether turnover and costs are both shown net or gross. The Rate of Gross Profit might vary. However, there can be a significant difference in the insurable amount if the cover is a Gross Revenue cover, if that Gross Revenue is related to total receipts rather than just commission.

The degree of underinsurance that might arise if gross receipts rather than the profit/commission thereon should be insured could be very significant. Insurers have in the past confirmed that Gross Revenue policy wordings should be applied strictly and significant shortfalls have been suffered by insured businesses that have only insured margin (but reflected Gross Revenue in their annual accounts).

Declaration Linked policies (discussed in chapter 3) do not allow for underinsurance but the declarations submitted to insurers still need to accurately reflect the underlying insurable amount.

The policy wording implicitly assumes that physical damage will give rise to corresponding Turnover losses within a defined period, such losses effectively commencing as at the date of the damage. Whilst this is generally a reasonable proposition, it need not be so.

In one case, a business developing software for use in equipment found in the majority of UK homes enjoyed an income stream based upon royalties to be generated in the future founded upon technical advances achieved today. The royalties currently being received related to yesterday's technical advances. Even were the Premises to be raised to the ground by fire and to remain so for two years, income would be unlikely to be affected.

The consequences of Damage would result in royalties being depressed in the medium-term when the next generation of products should have been earning royalties but in fact do not exist. A turnover loss would not arise within a twelve or even twenty-four-month Maximum Indemnity Period and potentially would never crystallise quickly enough for a claim to be submitted. That could be difficult to explain to the businessman who has paid a premium in respect of the business for many years.

In such a situation, it might be more meaningful to relate loss to the sales value of the loss of production time rather than requiring a turnover shortfall to crystallise.

There is a parallel with businesses generating income from annual subscriptions which may not be in jeopardy until a future period. The future subscriptions for that period may not be secure if work to support them is not being done in the aftermath of an incident. The point is also relevant to the distillation of whisky. A fire at the distillery may not affect turnover for twelve years, bottles being drawn from bonded store to supply to the market until that time. Rather than provide a policy written on a standard gross profit basis, such businesses benefit more from policies written on the basis of a Loss of Output, translating the production loss into a financial loss on an agreed basis. Pre claim discussion as to how this should be calculated is always beneficial.

Insurers can be satisfied that the basis on which premiums are received is consistent with the basis on which any future claim would be presented. Estimated Maximum Loss calculations can then be carried out with more certainty.

The insured person benefits from knowing the basis on which a claim will be paid.

Increased Cost of Working

The policy allows for additional costs to be incurred in order to prevent a Loss of Gross Profit arising, but not exceeding the amount that would be payable if the latter did transpire. This is known as the ‘economic limit’. Overtime working by staff to avoid a loss of Turnover is a good example. It would be curious if the insured business was not provided with such cover - Gross Profit losses are invariably more significant than Increased Costs of Working that might be incurred to avoid them.

In the detailed wording, the increased cost cover is set out as item 1(b), the Gross Profit cover being item 1(a). On the policy schedule, it would be normal to show only the Gross Profit cover as item 1, but this does not mean that the increased cost cover is absent.

It is important to note that the economic limit is considered with reference to the profit at risk from the insurer’s point of view i.e. that presenting itself within the Maximum Indemnity Period selected by the insured business under the policy. It is not restricted to the precise transaction that the costs are supporting. The value of a customer account over the full Maximum Indemnity Period is the correct reference point.

Notwithstanding the need to consider the economics of any cost incurred within the insured period, the insured business may wish to take a longer-term view, particularly in terms of key customers. A relatively modest customer this year may represent a significant account for the future and there is nothing to stop the insured business contributing to a cost themselves were it to be in their interest to do so to reflect the benefit of that expenditure to the business after the end of the Maximum Indemnity Period.

There is no requirement in the business interruption policy for an insured person to let either the insurer or the loss adjuster know if an increased cost is being incurred - either the cost is economically laid out to stop a loss accruing, which solely and directly derives from the insured incident, or it is not. As an aside, this is also the position with Gross Profit losses, which would be claimable even if not formally quantified until the end of the indemnity period. That assumes the incident was nevertheless notified promptly and the loss properly mitigated.

In reality, it is greatly in the interest of the insured business to discuss all significant costs to be incurred in advance with insurers and/or loss adjusters. The latter will be liaising with the insured business on a frequent basis and a mitigation strategy developed such that in the majority of cases the advisability of incurring any particular cost would have been discussed prior to the monies being laid out.

In certain cases, the insured business may require the explicit support of the insurer prior to following a certain route. This is certainly the case with regards to television advertising, for example, for businesses that have historically not had to advertise and which do not have a budget representing the significant sums that such campaigns can cost. In practice, if the insurers and loss adjusters agree that a course of action makes sense and should be employed, it would not be normal for reimbursement of that increased cost to be restricted even if the cost subsequently proved to be strictly uneconomic.

This reflects an increasingly proactive role undertaken by insurers in supporting businesses following major incidents - watching from a distance and ultimately carrying out strict economic tests for costs and mitigation plans not previously discussed would be untenable. Of course, the insured person that does choose to keep the costs being incurred confidential will invite a strict retrospective economic appraisal.

A frank exchange of information between insurers/loss adjusters and the insured business facilitates interim payments post loss, as well as allowing that business to benefit from the previous experience of disaster management that insurers have.

It is relevant to refer again to the fact that not all consequences of insured incidents are admissible items under a business interruption cover. There can be a perception that any additional cost not addressed under the material damage policy must by definition be an Increased Cost to be dealt with in the business interruption claim. That is not so - to be an admissible Increased Cost the policy definition must be met. If, following a late delivery to a customer, a contractual liquidated payment is required, then that would not constitute an Increased Cost. It would derive primarily because of an historic contract and not in respect of a decision taken solely to avoid a future reduction in turnover. The fact that a future loss of turnover would no doubt accrue if the historic contractual requirement was not met would merely be incidental. It would not arise directly as a result of Damage. Such a cost can be insured under a Fines and Penalties extension.

It is possible to expand the Increased Cost cover to remove the economic limit, (Additional Increase in Cost of Working cover) and this is discussed in chapter 6, along with an indication of the sort of circumstances where such additional cover might be advisable.

Savings

Finally, the policy allows for the deduction of 'any sum saved' in respect of costs that would have been paid or payable but for the incident. These represent saved variable costs below the Gross Profit line that would have been incurred had there not been the operation of an insured peril. A simple example would be the fact that there will be a reduction in the variable electricity charge if a machine is not running.

The application of savings merely reflects the principle of indemnity. The only costs that would be deducted as variable costs represent those cash flows not deducted from turnover in defining gross profit that would not have occurred but for the incident but which in fact declined because of it. An insured person, in deducting costs from turnover to define gross profit, is assuming that such costs will decline in proportion to turnover, and asserting that such costs will definitely be deducted from turnover in the event. The risk of the assumption lies with the insured business. The only costs deducted as savings are those that do actually reduce. The risk of assuming significant savings, therefore, lies with the underwriter in carrying out his Estimated Maximum Loss calculation.

All Risks/Perils Cover

There are essentially two ways in which the scope of cover can be addressed. An All Risks policy can be arranged which essentially provides for cover from external accidental causes subject to specified exclusions. Alternatively, a specified list of insured events (perils) can be listed and these will form the basis of the cover. Generally speaking, the All Risks approach will be preferable to avoid inadvertently omitting perils.

The detailed operation of the All Risks (or contingency) policy compared to a perils cover is outside the scope of this book, particularly as the decision as to the basis of the cover will be taken in respect of the material damage cover in the first instance.

As far as the business interruption is concerned, it is merely suggested that there be a consistent approach taken to that adopted under the material damage cover unless there is a particularly good reason for not doing so. If the Material Damage section of a perils policy is expanded to include theft or malicious damage, for example, the need to expand the business interruption cover on the same basis might be overlooked. There have been numerous claims in the past where this was precisely the case. An insured business assumed that both physical damage and ensuing loss of profit following a theft, for example, would be covered, but a close reading of the policy revealed that the material damage cover was sufficient but not the business interruption.

An extension of material damage cover is often effected without detailed consideration of whether the business interruption cover should likewise be expanded.

A parallel can be found in the insurance of books and records or archived documents. Many professional firms archive files and papers off site, frequently retaining them for six years or sometimes longer. The requirement to retain the paperwork might emanate from tax authorities, customers (who require the retention of audit trails), professional bodies, a quality control/evidential perspective, or from other sources.

It is often the case that the material damage cover will be extended to include documents at third party storage locations. However, the business interruption may be overlooked. A fire or other damage at the third party site could occur which would not allow for the operation of a business interruption cover, as that third party location would probably not be included within the standard definition of Premises within the schedule.

It may not be necessary to arrange for business interruption cover in relation to Damage to such documents, but if this is the intention of both the insured person and the insurer, then either the definition of Premises requires to be altered or a protocol agreement in respect of a specific third party location is needed. In essence, the simple recommendation is consistency. Policies set-up with a material damage cover written on an All Risks basis and a more restrictive business interruption cover written on a Perils basis can lead to dissatisfaction at claims time.

3. Declaration Linked Policies

Most commercial material damage policies contain average provisions. If a building should be insured for £1,000,000 and is insured for £500,000 then only 50% of a claim would be met by the policy (assuming reinstatement). In many cases policies provide some leeway and do not apply underinsurance if the sum insured under the policy represents more than 85% of the value at risk even if it remains marginally inadequate (full underinsurance would be applied if the sum insured were to be less than 85%).

The situation can be quite different with business interruption policies. Whether a policy is written on the basis of Gross Income/Revenue or on the basis of Gross Profit cover there are essentially two approaches that can be taken.

Policies can be purchased that allow for proportionate reduction if the level of the gross profit represents less than the gross profit at risk (non-Declaration Linked policies).

Alternatively, a Declaration Linked policy can be arranged. In this case, the policy schedule will refer to Estimated Gross Profit rather than merely Gross Profit (or Estimated Gross Revenue rather than merely Gross Revenue). The great advantage of these policies is that they do not allow for any underinsurance. Indeed, a Declaration Linked policy allows the insured business to claim up to 133.3% of the sum insured.

Under a standard Gross Profit wording, underinsurance is catered for according to the Association of British Insurers standard wordings as follows:

"[The operative clause precedes this paragraph]... *Provided that if the sum insured for this item be less than the sum produced by applying the Rate of 46 Gross Profit to the Annual Turnover (or to a proportion of the increased multiple thereof where the Maximum Indemnity Period exceeds twelve months), the amount payable should proportionately be reduced."*

This contrasts with a parallel wording in respect of Declaration Linked policies as follows:

"The liability of the insurer shall in no case exceed, in respect of Gross Profit, 133.3% of the Estimated Gross Profit stated herein, in respect of each other item 100% of the sum insured stated herein, nor in the whole the sum of 133.3% of the Estimated Gross Profit and 100% of the sums insured of other items."

Estimated Gross Profit is defined as:

"The amount declared by the insured to the insurer as representing not less than the Gross Profit which it is anticipated will be earned by the business during the financial year most nearly concurrent with the period of insurance (or a proportionately increased multiple thereof where the Maximum Indemnity Period exceeds twelve months)."

At face value, there is no apparent reason why any insured business would wish to take out a business interruption cover that is not declaration linked. To do so would be to actively court the risk of underinsurance. It is particularly relevant to observe that premiums for declaration linked policies do not vary significantly from those of non declaration linked covers, if at all.

The mechanics of the declaration linked cover involve the submission of an anticipated gross profit figure. A proportionate adjustment of premium based on the difference between the final confirmation and the initial estimate is then made. The position of the insurer is, therefore, protected in terms of receiving the correct premium, assuming that the end of year declarations are properly submitted. The insured business benefits from the absence of underinsurance.

There are some policies that are **not** written on an Estimated Gross Profit basis that nevertheless involve the submission of declarations (at the end of the policy period for premium refund purposes). Confusion might arise, if an insured business assumes that the policy is declaration linked when it is not.

The policy wording will make the position clear and should be relied upon in preference to the existence of declarations.

There can be a temptation, in the absence of underinsurance, to pay less attention to the calculation of Gross Profit than is appropriate. An empirical survey of claims dealt with by business interruption loss adjusters (conceding that this was not a formal statistical review) suggested that between 40% and 60% of Estimated Gross Profit losses would have been subject to underinsurance provisions had they been written on a Gross Profit basis.

The consequence of a significant under declaration is potentially more serious than mere underinsurance. The initial estimate of Gross Profit is made within the context of Utmost Good Faith. A significant under declaration may constitute a breach of Utmost Good Faith and the underlying policy cover could be voidable in such a case.

On occasions, where the Estimated Gross Profit is shown to be significantly less than that which should have been disclosed, insurers have (acting on legal advice) rejected claims and declared policies void. Where the under declaration is deliberate there is little scope for argument. If the under declaration is merely inadvertent, the insurer's entitlement to avoid the policy is less clear cut.

A deliberate under declaration would arise where a business, to cut its costs sets the level of Gross Profit in accordance with the level of premium that it feels comfortable paying. In so doing it will be aware that the Gross Profit figure declared to the insurer could be significantly depressed. The exposure that underwriters would presume existed could be significantly lower than was actually the case, and the Estimated Maximum Loss calculations could be flawed as a result.

Inadvertent under declaration might arise out of a misunderstanding of the definition of Gross Profit - a declaration of Gross Profit after deduction of wages, for example, (see the discussion of Gross Profit below) is not uncommon, notwithstanding that it is normally inappropriate. Insurers would still be concerned as their Estimated Maximum Loss calculations would be based upon significantly smaller figures than those presenting themselves in reality.

Regardless of the fact that they would be deprived of premium due (or at least the interest over the year's delay when the correct level is ultimately

confirmed), it might be that, if a risk was presented at the correct level initially, then the underwriters would not have provided cover at all.
It is important to realise that the 133.3% is a maximum claimable amount. It in no way depresses the level of profit that should form the basis of the estimate. If a business generates annual profit of £13,300,000, the estimate should declare profit of that level. It would be incorrect to declare profit at £10,000,000 notwithstanding that the 133.3% would increase the profit to the correct level. Underwriters would still be misled as to the size of the risk presenting itself.

A review of business interruption claims over a number of years confirms that **80% of the underlying business interruption policies are not Declaration Linked**. It is, therefore, suggested that this is likely to be an issue for a high proportion of insured businesses.

4. Business Issues

Overview

Insurance is about the unforeseen. Arranging cover which anticipates a specific anticipated scenario, or type of scenario is very dangerous. Almost certainly an unanticipated event will occur which will highlight a business issue that perhaps was too obvious even to have been identified but for a claim.

It is, therefore, difficult to set out a complete listing of risks that present themselves for different industry types. What is possible is to group together common practical issues that present themselves at claims time and these have been captured in three categories, namely management issues, physical issues and aspects arising from the nature of the business. Whilst such categorisation might be less ideal than summaries by industry, the latter could only be offered from a classroom perspective whereas the observations made below are founded upon actual claims experiences.

Management Issues

Team Competence

A very significant issue that will dictate the extent to which a business is able to mitigate a loss arising is the competence of the management team. A good team will produce an exceptionally rapid response to an incident and mitigate the interruption beyond reasonable expectations:

On one occasion, a business producing porcelain tableware and ornaments suffered a fire exactly one week prior to a factory tour to be undertaken by the Her Majesty the Queen. Unsurprisingly, Her Majesty was not to carry out the tour alone but would be accompanied by a large group of press reporters and photographers.

Whilst the fire only affected part of the Premises, the negative impact of press reporting on the degree of damage (which was not apparent from the perimeter of the site and which had not been fully appreciated in local press reports immediately after the incident), would have been severely detrimental.

Acting with decisiveness, the business insured constructed an elevated wooden walkway (fully enclosed) through the damaged zone along which Her Majesty and her entourage subsequently passed such that the degree of damage was not apparent.

The ensuing loss of turnover related only to the depression in productive capacity that the damage to the plant and equipment had caused. Overtime working was arranged to deal with this and repairs expedited to ensure as rapid a return to normality as possible. These costs, along with those expended to build the walkway, were dealt with as Increased Costs of Working.

Following any sort of incident, a loss of turnover can essentially derive from only one of two sources. Either there is an inability on the insured business to produce goods, or there is a disinclination on the part of customers to purchase them. The example just cited falls in the former category. Business interruption claims which derive from a depression in productive capacity tend to be very significantly smaller than those which arise from customer dissatisfaction. They can be dealt with through overtime or shift working or possibly subcontracting. In those situations once capacity is reinstated, the problem goes away.

The opposite is true if the customers are let down to any significant degree. Even when the productive facilities are reinstated, it may take many years for the customer base to be rebuilt. This could run for a long period after expiry of the Maximum Indemnity Period insured under the business interruption policy.

Commonly, there are two phases to a business interruption loss. Firstly, there is the period during which there is a depression in capacity pending the completion of repairs/replacement. There is then a tail to the claim whilst turnover is built-up to its previous level. The relationship between these two periods is exponential. An initial downtime of one day might produce an impact at least requiring overtime working for say two weeks. A downtime of one week might produce an impact of three months. One month's downtime could produce an impact for the following six to nine months. The impact of being down for between six and twelve months is likely to affect a business for several years.

The precise effect varies from business sector to business sector, a significant factor being the frequency with which customers visit the Premises. A customer might never use a newsagent again after calling daily for as little as a week. That same customer shopping for a three-piece suite might return after a week to a showroom closed the previous weekend. Only that proportion of the potential customer base seeking to make a purchase in the immediate aftermath of an insured incident would be dissatisfied.

There are other instances that could be cited which demonstrate what is possible to achieve with focused decisive action. Buildings that would ordinarily take ten months to construct have been erected in as little as six (where significant influence, commercial or otherwise, can be exerted both on the local authority, building contractors, machinery manufacturers etc.).

Where buildings have been raised to the ground in flashover fires, (but plant and machinery can still be cleaned/repaired instead of being replaced) temporary structures have been erected over key plant and machinery within the demised perimeter. Production has then continued even while the replacement building is erected around it.

If on-site mitigation is not possible, managed subcontracting, leasing facilities from other businesses for nightshift working, or other off site options have been successfully arranged in the past.

The optimum result may not be achieved, if there is reticence on the part of junior or middle management in particular to make decisions which are in the best interest of the business but which might have not been explicitly approved by loss adjusters. This may be a reflection of a negative corporate culture which might drive individuals to do nothing rather than try and do something for the best which does not prove to work out as anticipated.

Loss adjusters aspire to empower the insured business to make the right decisions after a claim and, when they succeed, the best results are achieved. Repeatedly, however, indecisiveness arises too often if management are driven by a fear of failing to maximise the insurance claim rather than a positive focus on the business. Usually, what is right for the business will also be right for insurers.

There are occasions where a business may decide, for example, not to place an order for the repair to a piece of plant because it wishes to take a strategic view in the long-term. Such an approach may not be a problem as long as it is discussed in advance and an alternative notional approach to the calculation of loss agreed. Such an understanding is critical, as a failure to mitigate, irrespective of any terms and conditions in a specific insurance policy, would debar a claim on the basis of common law.

It is usually obvious to loss adjusters and insurers, based on their previous claims experience, if there is undue delay in either designing a mitigation strategy or in executing it. A lack of openness in advising that the longer-term is being reviewed may otherwise create unnecessary suspicion and difficulty.

In the worst cases, the failure to mitigate arises for unsatisfactory reasons and can be associated with strange circumstances giving rise to the claim in the first place.

As well as overstated caution and a deliberate disinclination to deal with Damage, it is the case that some insured businesses have less commercial acumen than others. It is a truism to suggest that experiencing an insured event does not improve the basic competence that the insured person has to begin with. The level of incompetence is an aspect of the risk that underwriters took on at inception. Whereas the driven management team will massively mitigate a potential exposure, the inept team will explode it out of all proportion.

On one occasion, a business involved in a niche area of desktop publishing suffered a theft of all of its computers. (It was realised with hindsight that placing a sign over the doorway of the relevant building advising would be thieves that the 'IT studio' was within might not have been the wisest approach.) Insurers placed the business in funds to replace the hardware within seven working days, the insured having undertaken in a meeting with loss adjusters on the day of the incident to immediately replace all of the key pieces of equipment to continue to service the customers.

Despite agreeing to simply effect replacement, the insured business, in fact, decided that the system could be improved by purchasing slightly different equipment and by altering configurations. In aspiring to gain a long-term benefit (which in itself is no bad thing) alternative equipment was purchased that proved to be incompatible with both other purchases and equipment which was not stolen. Significant difficulties were experienced in configuring the system and loading all of the relevant software such that there was a total downtime of around one month. The majority of the customers published monthly if not weekly titles and all of them, therefore, had to source an alternative supplier at least in the short-term. Many of the customers that went elsewhere simply did not return.

This business had not failed to mitigate its loss as a deliberate decision. The actions that were taken were well intentioned and the goal was to produce a business benefit by what was done. Despite this, the business became insolvent after the end of the Maximum Indemnity Period, only lasting that long because of the support of the insurance policy.

This situation is unusual in that the incompetent insured, generally speaking, will not be able to trade his business to make a profit. Such businesses tend not to exist for long enough to make a business interruption claim, let alone one of significance. There are niche areas, however, where the incompetent businessman is able to make a healthy living, albeit less so than many others would achieve.

The issue of management competence is fundamental as this is what drives many other areas that risk managers, surveyors and underwriters consider. Disaster recovery plans are a good example. A competent team will have drawn up some form of disaster recovery plan. This reflects a recognition that such plans are an essential part of the directors' duties to protect the assets of the business as explicitly required by Companies Act 1985. Business plans tend not to be so specifically detailed that they give step by step guidance in the event of any particular unforeseen event (such a plan could run to many dozens of volumes), but can be useful in setting out parameters.

Various surveys have been undertaken in the past by firms of chartered accountants, among others, seeking to establish a correlation between the existence of disaster recovery plans and the extent of business interruption losses arising after insured events. Such surveys can be misleading. It is almost unheard of in an initial meeting with loss adjusters after an insured event has occurred, for the managing director to draw the attention of the meeting to the relevant page in the disaster recovery plan that can provide guidance.

What happens is that the meeting effectively constitutes a focused brainstorm session that marries the knowledge of the business that the directors have with the knowledge of the operation of the insurance policy that the brokers and loss adjusters have. That there is some correlation between mitigation of business interruption losses and the existence of disaster plans, therefore, is an indirect one. It merely reflects the fact that the competent team is more likely to have produced a plan but will also be capable of designing a practical and effective mitigation strategy as an independent facet.

Again, the competence of management will dictate the extent to which health and safety issues are properly addressed, business risks covered off and the business operated generally, as well as the response to a disaster whether this comprises an insurance event or not.

The challenge for the underwriter and broker, of course, is to be able to identify which insured businesses are run by a competent team and which are not. Invariably, there is a mix of individuals on the board of any business who will sit at various places between those two poles.

The identification of the less competent insured can only be inferred indirectly. A properly laid out and orderly shop floor is one indicator of competence. Timely production of financial information is another. It is not uncommon for businesses to produce only rudimentary or incomplete budgets and forecasts (particularly if cash rich and not dependent upon banks or other third parties) - even management accounts may not be produced on a monthly basis. Whilst there are many businesses run extremely effectively who do not produce this information, in the majority of cases it is difficult to see how proper control can be exercised without an effective financial environment.

Ultimately, the assessment of competence may have to rest upon a subjective assessment of the individuals being presented. Brokers and underwriters will have their own methods of assessing competence on the basis of many years of experience.

It is worth observing that brokers frequently encounter difficulty obtaining relevant and timely financial information to allow sums insured to be properly assessed and for declarations to be made under stock and Estimated Gross Profit covers. Generally speaking, if an insured business is reluctant or unable to produce basic financial information at inception or renewal, then there is no basis to conclude that such information will be any easier to obtain if a claim is made.

The significance in identifying the incompetent insured is that he will need both more expansive cover and a significantly longer Maximum Indemnity Period as part of his policy protection.

It is accepted that there is a sales challenge inherent in this suggestion. Advising an insured that a long Maximum Indemnity Period is desirable in itself is easy enough. Explaining that the suggestion arises because one or more members of staff are assessed as incompetent is less easy.

Key Personnel

The ongoing need for businesses to reduce costs generally has paralleled an increasing focus on process efficiency. To some extent, specialisation has meant that the head count at a managerial level (as well as in the workforce generally) is lower than it once was. More specifically, expert knowledge may exist only in the minds of very few and sometimes only one individual.

On one occasion, a pharmaceutical company suffered a fire, and established subcommittees to manage the response to the incident dealing with the building, the plant and machinery, the customers, etc., to produce manageable working groups. The product involved some fairly advanced chemistry and was manufactured using specialised equipment. Very often some of the main contacts within customers were also technical people and, therefore, the technical staff within the insured business found themselves pulled in many directions. In particular, the technical director found himself appointed to almost every subcommittee.

Loss adjusters advised the insurer involved that there was a reasonable chance that this individual would not be able to cope and would either suffer catastrophic fatigue over a three to six month period or might alternatively decide to leave the business.

This highlighted an enormous reliance on the technical knowledge of one individual and this is not unusual for businesses involved in specialist areas such as the medical industry, or in the case of electronics, or IT intensive businesses.

A parallel can be drawn with a business run in an autocratic manner where delegation is uncommon. In that situation a bottleneck in decision-making is invariably going to arise which will produce delay and this will usually diminish the effectiveness of the mitigation strategy and increase the loss should a claim occur. Again, there are exceptions to every rule, and the truly gifted autocratic director may be able to achieve a more rapid response through fear of failure in a short-term on the part of staff than a combination of the minds of many would achieve. Generally speaking, however, the latter approach tends to produce the best results.

On one occasion, the senior partner of a professional firm became very depressed after the occurrence of an insured incident. Concerned that he was no longer fit to act as senior partner, he demoted himself to the level of Associate, subsequently resigning from the firm. An exacerbation of loss caused by the mental deterioration of the partner followed.

The significance of few key personnel speaks to a longer Maximum Indemnity Period.

For completeness, it should be noted that the reference to key men in this context is quite different from taking out a key man insurance policy which addresses the sudden death, for example, of a critical individual. That is different from an over reliance on individuals who have personally suffered no adverse effect following an insured peril impacting the business.

Outsourced Functions

Outsourcing is more fashionable at some times than at others, but is always relevant to identify and consider when designing the business interruption insurance programme.

Outsourcing is often an overt aspect of the production process - passing textiles out to a dye house, for example, or metal components to an electroplating contractor. Whilst these require consideration in respect of suppliers extensions, they tend to be readily identifiable, in the majority of cases. Where the subcontracting relates to something other than a production process, the situation can be quite different.

An awareness, however, that the business has taken the outsource decision is important. Consider the situation where a business factors its invoices. When an invoice is sent to a customer, it will be copied to the invoice factors, who will pay a very significant proportion of the face value of the invoice immediately. The customer is advised on the face of the invoice to then pay the full amount to the factor. The excess over the immediate payment may be retained by the factor as its profit. Such an approach assists cash flow and can help reduce the costs of chasing debt.

Unfortunately, if there is an insured event which stops production and invoices stop being despatched to customers, there will be an immediate cessation of income. Generally speaking, in the month or so after an insured event occurs, most (non-cash) businesses will still continue to receive cash from those customers invoiced in the previous month. Whilst in due course cash flow will come to a halt without the support of interim payments from insurers, the immediacy of the cash flow cessation for a company factoring its invoices can be very serious.

Insurers have to be allowed a reasonable period of time to investigate the circumstances of a claim, either directly or through loss adjusters, and to consider the availability of policy cover. If there are unsatisfactory aspects to a claim, or if it represents an incident of arson, when any involvement of the insured person has to be discounted, then the liability admission can be very much deferred. If the cause of an incident is not immediately apparent, then further investigation is inevitably required.

The cash flow position is not something that can be insured against. It is, however, worth appreciating in advance. The availability of Additional

Increase in Cost of Working cover cannot help accelerate the liability decision but would provide the comfort to the insured company that necessary decisions can be taken to achieve the best result for the business without the fear of the economic limit applying. Loss adjusters would also be able to agree that the correct decisions were being taken, subject to the acceptance of liability being outstanding.

Insurers are covering Gross Profit rather than cash flow and in principle impecuniosity is not something that insurers are bound to deal with. Losses that flow from impecuniosity under a business interruption policy by definition are not flowing from Damage and, therefore, are not specifically brought under the ambit of the cover. In most practical cases they are not relevant to the calculation of settlement. Insurers would be bound to pay the full amount of the loss arising where there is an insured cause (fire, for example) and an uninsured cause (competitor gossip about the fire, for example) arising coterminously from the same event. An inability to specifically separate out the impact of the two (and this is usually impossible) would mean that insurers have to deal with the whole amount. This is to be contrasted with a situation where an excluded cause runs coterminously with an insured cause. In that case, if the effects cannot be split out then insurers may be advised that they need pay nothing.

Group Strategy

The above three issues (team competence, key personnel, and outsourced functions) relate primarily to the length of the Maximum Indemnity Period. In contrast, group strategy towards inter company trading is relevant to the calculation of gross profit and claims difficulties that may arise.

At the extremes, there are two bases on which subsidiary companies within a group might trade with each other. Either subsidiaries will, in the first instance, source raw material/components from other group companies in preference to external firms, or they will primarily source product on the basis of best price whether that be from an internal or external supplier. The advantage of the former approach is that profit is retained within the group to the maximum extent. The disadvantage is that such an approach can encourage complacency and a failure to properly control the cost base through reduced competition.

The issue of inter company trading becomes relevant as far as an insurance policy is concerned in two respects: the declaration of values at risk as far as stock is concerned, and the basis of inter company profit generated through the year.

As far as the inter company profit is concerned, consider the following:

	Subsidiary A	**Subsidiary B**
	£	**£**
Revenue	1.50	2.00
Cost	1.00	1.50
Profit	50	50

At the end of the year, when the above two subsidiaries report their financial results, subsidiary A will advise revenue of £1.50 for each widget sold to subsidiary B and B will likewise record that as a cost. However, total revenue for the two subsidiaries would be £3.50. This is a nonsense, as the revenue to the group, represented by B selling the product to the external customer is £2.00 not £3.50. As far as the group is concerned, the purchase cost was £1.00 and the revenue is £2.00 and that is that.

To ensure that sets of accounts for groups of companies (group accounts) only reflect the external trading position, it is necessary to make some adjustments (consolidation adjustments) to the total of the individually reported results from the subsidiaries. In the above example, the total revenue reported by A and B of £3.50 would be reduced to £2.00 and the combined cost reduced from £2.50 to £1.00. As the reduction is £1.50 to both revenue and cost there is no impact on profit but it prevents an artificial impression of financial robustness merely by inflating turnover through selling from one subsidiary to another.

Given that consolidation adjustments will be carried out as a matter of routine at year end, it may be convenient to ask subsidiaries to make regular insurance declarations in accordance with their normal financial disciplines. The premium due for the group can then be adjusted with reference to the consolidation adjustment schedules. The advantage of this approach is that the insured business is not encumbered with any onerous special requirements over and above the financial disciplines normally observed whilst the premium still reflects the trading position, net of inter company trading. The disadvantage of this annual retrospective adjustment is that an accurate division of the premium between the various subsidiaries may not be possible albeit a reasonably accurate split can still be made. Some accuracy will be sacrificed for convenience.

A difficulty, as far as claims are concerned, presents itself when there is a fire which affects subsidiary B in the example above. For each widget destroyed it may be that a stock claim for £1.50 will be presented and a business interruption claim of 50p. The loss adjuster in that situation (assuming that the cover is written on a group basis) would advise that the stock claim should properly be stated at £1.00 (the external cost to the group). The Gross Profit would represent external revenue less the £1.00 external cost i.e. also £1.00. The loss adjuster's total calculated losses will be £2.00 exactly in accordance with the claim.

However, consider a situation where the loss happens just prior to financial year end. The stock claim may have crystallised prior to the balance sheet date but the business interruption loss will still be in the future. Whilst overall the revenue figure may not be in dispute, the finance director of the subsidiary company, whose annual salary package may be dependent on divisional results, is unlikely to be happy to take the £1.00 for the stock claim rather than the £1.50 submitted as this will impact upon him financially in the short-term.

The same situation can arise where there is a more modest insured event which produces a stock loss only. In that situation the rejection of a £1.50 claim in favour of a £1.00 proposed adjustment can again produce difficulty in so far as the figures impact the particular subsidiary or division.

Problems have been encountered in the past where a group finance director or risk manager has accepted the logic of adjustments needed to reflect the overall group position, but has not communicated the issue effectively to the subsidiary managers/directors properly. If there is a claim, misunderstandings can arise leading to disputes that could have been avoided.

It will be appreciated that the above hypothetical example involves only two subsidiary companies. There have been cases in the past where a reasonably sized manufacturing group contains many subsidiary companies, each carrying out different processes such that a dozen or more companies in some cases might be sending product to each other before delivery to an external customer. In practice, one subsidiary simply might not know what the cost of manufacture in the originating subsidiary is. Unless this has been discussed in a practical way in advance of a claim, there is the potential for a loss adjuster or claims handler to inadvertently propose settlement which includes some element of inter company profit. Alternatively, there may be a significant delay whilst cost bases in other subsidiary companies are established.

In many situations the selling price passed from subsidiary to subsidiary increases as more manufacturing processes are carried out and value added to the product. It might be considered appropriate, therefore, to agree that lost revenue within the group itself should be accepted as the basis for a claim notwithstanding that a group policy subsists. The advantage in this approach for insurers is that premium can be calculated on a basis which will be known to be consistent with that on which the claim will be calculated.

The lifetime of the claim may also be shortened through not having to involve other subsidiary companies and insurers' liabilities when a claim occurs can be quantified more quickly. The advantage for the insured business is that a considerable amount of management time might be saved and delay avoided if a protocol can be established to allow for a convenient and practical basis of measuring quantum.

In the absence of any specific agreement, the position is that inter company losses would not be claimable. Loss external to the group would need to be demonstrated. Pre loss discussion will reflect the merits of any particular approach and avoid expectation difficulties when a claim is made.

There is a separate issue from all of the above, and that centres around the definition of cost. Subsidiaries are likely to have added overhead costs to the base value of the stock and the issues that can arise depending on the nature of the costs so included are discussed in chapter 8.

Physical Aspects

The fundamental issue of correctly defining Premises has been discussed above. Specific points that have presented themselves in the claims process in the past have been grouped below under the headings of the site itself, the buildings and the contents thereof.

Site

Businesses that have the benefit of occupying a location with a reasonable amount of empty space which is not taken up by buildings, car parks, etc., within the curtillage, have a much better chance of continuing to operate from that site following the operation of an insured peril. There will be room for temporary power generation units or refrigeration units or any other specialist equipment that may be required. Temporary facilities in terms of offices etc. can also be erected.

The level of sophistication that temporary facilities have now reached is significant. In the past, in the case of private schools, for example, whole temporary villages have been created with libraries, dining halls, kitchens and dormitories linked by a network of pavements with low level external lighting and security facilities.

The advantages of remaining on the existing site are obvious. Suppliers and customers know where to find the business, stationery does not have to be produced with new addresses, not all of the plant/office accommodation may have to be relocated and all of the additional logistical difficulties that relocation requires on top of the problems that the insured event has already raised do not have to be dealt with.

To move a manufacturing business of any reasonable size could easily cost £100,000, and that assumes that there are no special requirements unique to the business.

There have been a number of claims in the past where even modest claims have benefited from available space on-site. Consider water or potential smoke damage to stock that may look similar to the layman (foam components in a three-piece suite manufacturer, small component parts in automotive supply businesses, lace napkins are all good examples). Space is required to potentially take all of this stock and store it whilst any potential smoke or water damage is assessed. Doing this on-site is a lot more convenient than doing it away from the premises.

There have been a number of occasions in the past where potentially affected stock has been removed to an alternative warehouse for subsequent inspection whilst the shelving at the Premises is cleaned ready to accept replacement supplies to allow the business to continue trading. There is a significant danger that the day-to-day operation of the business will mean that the stock assessment process does not get underway for some time. Potentially it may not be completed before the end of the Maximum Indemnity Period (and will be a drain on management time until that point). Whilst such a danger is not removed if the business remains on-site, the proximity of the stock and the greater convenience in arranging its assessment reduces the likelihood of this happening.

The shape of the site and the nature of the boundaries are also important to consider. Canals along one or more sides of the perimeter, for example, may provide a ready source of water in the case of fire. Incidentally, restricted access to the Premises from one or more directions may suggest the need to consider a denial of access extension.

Canals in particular may also indicate a need to consider cover for failure of utilities. The only places where utility companies can move their pipes/cabling from the one side of a canal to the other will be at the bridging points. Depending on the number of bridges in the immediate environment, a significant number of utility providers, alongside the likes of cable television suppliers, may have concentrated their services at these focal points. The pavements in such areas may be excavated with regularity to effect maintenance/repair/improvement works.

It is reasonable to suppose that the likelihood of a pick axe passing through a service cable will increase with the number of excavation events, the risk of utility failure increasing likewise.

Railway lines in the immediate vicinity may also indicate a need to consider a denial of access and loss of utility covers. Electrical cabling failures in particular are as likely to arise because a stone by a railway track has, over a period of time, penetrated a utility cable as a consequence of the vibration of passing trains, rather than because of cable damage by workmen.

It is important to consider the location not merely in terms of the physical boundaries, but also in terms of any non-physical limitations.

Whilst local authorities would not allow by design some of the mixed use industrial/residential areas that currently exist, such areas have arisen historically and may represent a particular threat to the ability of a business to work overtime to recover potential lost gross profit. Noise Abatement Orders may have been served by the local authority preventing the business operating outside reasonable working hours, depending on the amount of noise/traffic involved. It follows that if there is such a restriction then there will be a limit on a mitigation strategy that might otherwise be undertaken (providing a night shift, for example) and a longer Maximum Indemnity Period for such a business should be considered.

It is also the case that, if there are neighbours that are hostile to the existence of the business in its existing location, then more difficulty is going to be experienced in terms of planning permission (if required), post loss. Even if the neighbours are not antagonistic, the local authority itself may prefer to see the area occupied purely by residential premises, and this is more likely if the insured business is one of only few commercial operations in the vicinity.

Increasingly, previously industrial areas on the immediate outskirts of UK cities are being redeveloped by the construction of 'luxury' residential developments and the completion of significant numbers of such developments may produce a danger of a protracted and difficult planning issue post loss that did not previously exist.

For retail businesses, if they occupy their existing location because of the presence of another well known retailer then there is a risk that Damage to the Premises of the latter could produce an impact on the business potentially as severe as if the occupied Premises themselves were affected. In such cases a Loss of Attraction extension to the business interruption policy is advisable.

Buildings

To a significant extent, issues with regards to the construction of buildings have been considered in detail and authoritatively by others. In particular, combustible composite panels, the presence of asbestos, the existence of significant voids above suspended ceilings and the presence of non-standard methods of construction are difficulties that have presented themselves.

As far as the business interruption policy is concerned, the existence of these features is likely to mean reconstruction will be extended and that a longer Maximum Indemnity Period is going to be required. It may also be the case that Additional Increase in Cost of Working cover would be advisable. The latter will allow for significant incentivisation of builders/landlords in the event of an insured incident occurring. Whilst not specifically a business interruption issue, it is fairly common to find that debris removal cover is insufficient to deal with the very significant costs of removing asbestos or other hazardous or industrial waste. That should be addressed as part of the material damage cover - the Additional Increase in Cost of Working cover is not going to pickup material damage costs where the material damage insurance is inadequately arranged. It can of course still incentivise the process.

The absence of sprinklers highlights another issue, that of pre or post loss insurer requirements. A significant fire (or any other insured event), or the issue of policy cover to a substantial business for the first time, is likely to result in various improvements being suggested or required by the insurers. The installation of sprinklers following a fire is one example - the need to install fire suppression equipment on plant or improve security measures after theft are others. The requirement to install sprinklers post loss, either as part of the building structure or within stock racking, would not only present an unforeseen pressure on the cash flow of the business, but would potentially also extend the time taken to repair damage. The siting of water tanks, if required, might also be a practical problem.

If insurers require changes to be made which impact on the length of the reinstatement process, then the likely additional business interruption losses would usually be dealt with as part of the claim. Likewise, extended downtime and the resulting increased business interruption losses arising from the application of the local authorities clause would be included in any settlement.

These situations might be contrasted with delay in recommencing production as a consequence of the insured business voluntarily deciding to carry out improvements or to undertake work to permanently increase capacity. Any additional losses arising therefrom would not be covered.

Delay arising from work undertaken by contractors (observing their own professional or industry protocols and standards) beyond that strictly necessary is more difficult to comment definitively on. The precise circumstances presenting themselves would need to be considered.

Clearly, in all of the above scenarios, there is a need to ensure that all of the repair/reinstatement work arising from Damage is expedited in a timely manner. It will also assist if this can be dovetailed with any additional work undertaken by the insured business.

A significant issue as far as the design of a business interruption policy is concerned is the presence of listed status for a building. The need to involve government and/or heritage bodies in establishing the extent of damage and deciding the best method of repair/reinstatement introduces potential delay that should not be under estimated. Even initial cleaning of smoke damage may be an issue - an acceptable cleaning technique for stone work may not be acceptable for mosaic floors and stained glass windows, fabric, or wood. Potentially each will require a different approach. Delay will occur whilst the correct approach is established and inevitably further delay will arise through the need to co-ordinate the increased numbers of contractors and specialists on-site.

The historical importance of features of listed buildings will mean that expenditure will have to be incurred in restoring elements of buildings due to their historic significance that would not be contemplated on pure economic grounds.

There have been cases in the past where historic features that have not previously been known to have even existed have been identified during the repair/reinstatement basis. Delay in reinstating the business will arise whilst the relevant heritage body considers the significance of the new finding.

On one occasion, a public house dating back to the fifteenth century suffered direct fire damage and smoke spread. Subsequent stripping out of wooden facades revealed a long forgotten English civil war mural. To the untrained eye, it looked more like graffiti of the time, encouraging King Charles to 'large it up'. Significant delay to the reinstatement work arose whilst heritage bodies assessed the significance of this new find.

There are parallel, albeit more obvious, issues arising with older buildings that are not themselves listed. Thatched public houses are an obvious example in terms of fire risk. A disinclination to reinstate on a like for like basis may arise due to a fear of a repeat event, or a concern about future insurance premiums. Delay may result, impacting on the business interruption claim.

It may also be the case that the visual attraction of older buildings can only be replicated by an extended search for appropriate replacement materials. Whilst new methods of construction might replace the same footprint more quickly, restaurants might suffer a reduction in turnover on a permanent basis if the 'charm' of a destroyed building is lost. Guests/customers may go out of their way to reassure themselves that the building they were previously attached to has been properly restored.

The premium cost of accelerating specialist repairs can often be very much greater than increased costs necessary to accelerate more routine work. For a significant project, such costs might be uneconomic over a twelve or even twenty-four-month Maximum Indemnity Period. Additional Increase in Cost of Working cover might be of assistance in dealing with any uneconomic element after application of the standard Increase in Cost of Working cover.

Tenanted occupation of properties increases business interruption risk, as previously discussed. Even where a tenant is appreciated by the landlord, greater delay is likely to arise in arranging building repairs than with a freeholder, who also has gross profit issues to consider. Landlords are likely to be less willing to compromise the fabric of a listed building to reduce downtime for the benefit of a (possibly short to medium-term) tenant.

Tenancy, along with the presence of listed status, or attractive features such as thatching, are all likely to require at least a twenty-four-month Maximum Indemnity Period.

Contents

In some cases, it can be difficult to distinguish between the building and the plant and machinery. Consider a pit beneath a drop forge which will house interlaced oak beams to absorb the impact of the hammer blow when it comes down. Strictly, given that the pit set in the floor is immovable, it could be argued to be part of the building. On the other hand, the need for its existence is solely driven by the item of plant sitting above it and might be regarded therefore as an element of the plant and machinery. Such an issue may appear to be academic, but the cost of producing such pits can be a significant issue in assessing the adequacy of both the buildings and contents sums insured.

Some businesses, such as dairies, can have such complicated plant layouts that accurate distinction between buildings and contents can be very difficult to establish.

The above issue relates to clear identification of assets and valuation thereof as far as the material damage cover is concerned. For the business interruption cover, the existence of ancillary services or facilities required to support the production machinery is of significant concern. This includes the requirement for any specialist foundations, any underfloor drainage (which is not uncommon in the food production industry) or the need for any particular controlled airflow within buildings. All of these features would all make it more difficult to relocate to alternative premises to recommence production whilst repairs to the Premises are carried out.

There could be a limitation on the ability of the business to mitigate Gross Profit losses arising and a longer Maximum Indemnity Period is to be recommended. Additional Increase in Cost of Working cover may assist if this is set at a high enough level - even if an alternative building is identified which can be altered to allow production to recommence, the cost of so doing is likely to be very significant. An alternative risk approach would be to identify other businesses engaged in similar activities to agree reciprocal support in the event of a disaster.

Whilst the production plant may not require any specialist footing, there may be a requirement for extensive venting or height requirements, as is the case with polythene bag manufacturers, for example. In the case of specialist footings, the owners of alternative premises might be reluctant to allow significant alteration of their buildings, or if they did significant additional expense might present itself. The cost of reinstating the temporarily altered building could be significant.

Alternatively, there could be a particular layout required for the production of equipment, machines being sited close to each other in a particular configuration that requires a non-standard building footprint. On one occasion in the past, a significant incident occurred at a business producing direct mail material. This included the addition of perforations, glue, scratch and sniff panels etc. and required a footprint for a conveyor belt to pass paper along of a significantly greater size than might be anticipated. Difficulty in finding appropriate alternative premises ensued.

Any particular requirements with regards to production layout will suggest the need for a longer Maximum Indemnity Period and will represent a reduction in the ability of the business concerned to mitigate any loss presenting itself.

The nature of the stock held by a business is as relevant as the plant and machinery. Specialist storage requirements, such as refrigeration, might give rise to significant stock spoilage difficulties were there to be a failure in the electricity supply, for example. Regardless of the existence of any stock spoilage cover under the material damage policy, that would not be a matter to be dealt with under the business interruption cover. However, the shortage of raw materials, particularly if there is a long lead time in replacement, would be a significant issue for the business.

For businesses where there is a wide range of stock product lines, and particularly where many of those product lines are visually similar, the need to maintain consistency in terms of storage locations is important. Even experienced staff may become confused if, after an incident, the storage locations are radically rearranged (as will often be the case). If it is necessary to vacate site, a depression in the effectiveness of the business and a reduction in throughput will be exacerbated by unfamiliarity.

The use of patterns, dies or tools (or moulds in the pottery industry) is another significant issue requiring consideration. Some of the tooling may be extremely heavy requiring overhead winching to remove it from its storage location to the relevant machine that it serves. In such a situation, storage of the tooling close to the machine may be preferable. Again, a significant number of tools of similar design may require discipline in the manner of their storage and significant rearrangement of this can produce delay both in bringing the tooling to the machinery that it serves and also in ensuring that the correct tooling is being engaged.

Following an insured incident, alternative premises for the productive process might be identified, but necessary ancillary space, for example, to store tooling or the need for the establishment of the departments to prepare the tooling for use or cast operational moulds should not be overlooked. Where metal castings are produced via sand moulds, the mould production facility required can be extensive.

Whilst primarily a material damage issue, it is extremely common to find that the tooling has been significantly undervalued in establishing values at risk. Tooling relating to a product which is no longer part of the current range may have been omitted entirely from value at risk calculations. Alternatively, it may have been valued at internal cost if skilled engineers in-house have developed it. These costs could vary significantly with the external cost of requiring third parties to produce tooling after an incident.

Were external tool production to be required only for that proportion of tooling necessary for the immediate future, the additional cost of external firms solely to allow such tooling to be available for the benefit of turnover sooner than if developed in-house would comprise an acceptable increased cost. Additional Increased Cost of Working cover may be of significant assistance where irregular orders requiring expensive tooling are received, the economic limit otherwise presenting a potential problem.

With regards to the main items of plant and machinery, it is not uncommon for heavy pieces of plant to be installed before buildings are constructed. Dairies or chemical production plants are examples of businesses where the distinction between plant, machinery and buildings can be less obvious than normal. These situations challenge the ease of machine removal to any alternative site post Damage to mitigate a loss. The experience of claims is that a remarkable degree of success has been experienced in relocating even sensitive pieces of plant, but at the same time the cost of so doing has proven to be significantly higher than initially anticipated.

It is a good discipline, when setting sums insured at renewal, for businesses to consider replacement lead times not only for the main items of equipment, but also for replacement of the IT system including installation and configuration. If a building can be replaced in around ten months, any significant extension to that time for the commissioning of plant will indicate the need for a longer Maximum Indemnity Period.

Nature of Trade

Seasonal Business

The most extreme examples of businesses with a seasonal dependency are those manufacturing for specific events or periods of the year. Artificial Christmas trees, Easter eggs, suntan lotions and insect repellents for the holiday period are all good examples. Hotels may enjoy a marked seasonality. Whilst the fact that many businesses will produce a wide range of products rather than just those aimed at the specific seasonal market, thereby diluting the reliance on a particular sales window, this is not the case for everybody.

The danger is that the customer base will source other suppliers (they may have no alternative) if Damage cannot be dealt with quickly enough (by the arrangement perhaps of alternative production either on a reduced proportion of the original site, on another site, or through a subcontractor). Inevitably, if customers do source other suppliers, it will take such businesses at least one full subsequent season to try and build-up customer confidence again, or possibly two. An indemnity period of two or three years might be appropriate.

Additionally, the danger of incurring uneconomic increased costs is greater than for a business with trade and gross profit spread throughout the year. Expenditure can be incurred establishing alternative production facilities or for arranging subcontracting with other suppliers. However, where a non cyclical business would generate profit on the back of that expenditure throughout the Maximum Indemnity Period, there is a danger that a business dependent upon a particular event will miss the opportunity of supply and very low levels of turnover might be generated. The danger of exceeding the economic limit makes Additional Increase in Cost of Working cover advisable.

There are particular difficulties in respect of high fashion. This retail sector defies the traditional calendar year by having only two seasons - summer and winter. Orders may be placed anywhere between four and six months prior to the season beginning (compared to a month or less for some high street chains) with manufacturers who will then produce only to order to maintain scarcity of product and support premium prices.

A ram raid at the beginning of a season depriving a shop of all of its stock presents particular difficulties, as the supplier may well not retain buffer stock in its own warehouse. The only alternative is for the business in question to visit the premises of other retailers and to purchase their stock or alternatively to fill the shop with clothing readily available which may have a lesser premium and status.

If a business has to go out and buy replacement designer stock from other retailers, then, assuming that all businesses in the market place charge a similar selling price, the insured business will pay the equivalent of its own selling price to replace the stock. Depending on the margin achieved on selling price, the premium to be paid can be significant. This can impose a very heavy reliance on the increased cost cover and again the usefulness of Additional Increase in Cost of Working cover, which will meet the uneconomic element of costs not dealt with under the standard cover should not be under estimated.

In several claims in the past, the owners of fashion boutiques have maintained that they are unable to go out and purchase from other retailers as shops may concentrate on particular colour combinations for each season ('storylines'). The suggestion that stock from other suppliers should be bought may, therefore, be resisted if it undermines the storyline principle and detracts, in the mind of the insured business, from the ambience of the shop. What in effect such a business is saying is that, in practical terms, it does not believe that it can mitigate a loss at all if a theft or other insured peril affects the stock at an early point in the season.

Whether this is actually the case is not at issue here - the point is that such fundamental obstacles to loss mitigation should be drawn to the attention of the underwriter at inception/renewal so that there are no surprises at claims time. If the insurance cover is accepted on the basis that such a restriction on mitigation will arise then insurers can be satisfied that the appropriate premium has been paid for the additional risk presented.

Another example of a business that may experience difficulty mitigating a loss again concerns clothing. The point that it illustrates is generic. It is not uncommon at claims time for businesses with logos applied to buttons or sewn into fabric to resist releasing such clothing at less than full selling price (i.e. either through a salvage sale at the premises or by releasing product to salvage dealers). The business concerned may perceive that some customers will purchase the salvaged goods as opposed to the full price goods and that, therefore, releasing salvage will produce gross profit losses which will outweigh the benefit of any salvage proceeds.

Other businesses, regardless of any economic argument, suggest that the sale of their products other than in a premium environment will blemish their reputation.

Generally speaking, such businesses are comfortable with the product being released into Eastern European markets, but the return generated thereby is very much reduced as salvage dealers understandably have more restricted outlets and also higher costs to sell the salvage on.

It is advisable where the insured business perceives that there is a restriction on salvaging products for this to be raised with underwriters so that the matter can be resolved in advance of a claim arising. Underwriters may be happy to accept that salvage proceeds will be minimal (there have been cases involving varying degrees of damage to premium chocolate that has been sold on for pig food, for example), but clarification of that fact pre claim will assist. Consistency will be established between the basis on which the premium was set and the claim dealt with.

The Supply Chain

Supply

There may be a limitation in supplies. This can arise as a deliberate policy on the part of a supplier (as is the case with the designer retail clothing referred to above). It can be a product of capacity limitations on the part of the supplier. Or it could be a consequence of seasonal factors, where the products are simply not available throughout the year or are available, but only on the basis of long lead times.

All of these scenarios are of concern. Long lead times may be a particular concern where products are shipped from overseas, for example. An obvious response in such a situation would be to fly the product in rather than shipping it on the surface of the globe and dealing with the premium arising as an increased cost. In some cases (imports of heavy wood supplies, for example) the premium cost can be very significant.

It may be that a British distributor or wholesaler of products sourced overseas has buffer stock to avoid long lead times. However, it is a fact that for a major claim to be suffered by any business, it will need to suffer from a coincidental combination of circumstances. There have been cases in the past where a business has suffered a peril, which in the first instance may not be a major issue, but when there has been a subsequent event at the UK distributor of raw materials, the problem has then become catastrophic. This turn of events is a particular problem where there is one main UK distributor/wholesaler for product or one UK sales agent. Bottlenecks in the supply chain represent just as much risk as bottlenecks within the production cycle at the premises.

Demand

The corollary of restricted supply is restricted demand from customers. If a manufacturer produces assets that customers will require credit finance to purchase, it may be that the customers' capacity to buy is not based upon their perception purely of the quality of the product but on the availability of credit.

An increase in business interruption losses will arise if there is a delay in putting the product into the market place, or if the sales force may be unable to advise when exactly the product will again be available following a disaster. By the time the business is again able to supply, it may be that the customers have already used up all lines of finance to forward order from competitors. There have been cases where the product offered by the insured business is perceived as more efficient, reliable and less expensive but it will not be bought if the funds are not available.

Other Supply Chain Issues

Where a subcontractor is used to any great extent then a Suppliers Extension is advisable. Likewise, a significant reliance on a specific customer or customers will suggest a Customers Extension, or in the case of motor dealerships, for example, an extension relating to the premises of automobile manufacturers. These extensions are considered more fully in chapter 6, but it is worth stressing that increasing specialisation of businesses and a focus on reducing cost (including a reduction in buffer stocks held) does make any business more exposed to incidents occurring up and down the supply chain.

In one case, a business supplied the bulk of the internal apparatus for amplifiers which were sold to a customer who sourced the external housing box and some electrical components from another supplier. A fire suffered by that other supplier meant that the customer of the insured business placed no orders with them for an extended period of time - having surplus stock of interior components without the housing to place them in made no sense.

A significant incident at the premises of another supplier, or of a customer, may be as catastrophic in sales terms as an incident at the Premises themselves. Unless this aspect of the business has been identified and discussed, and dealt with through a special Customers of Suppliers extension then no claim could be made by the insured business if it occurs. Appreciating the basis on which a business secures its sales is the main driver for the business interruption policy.

Where suppliers provide outline production requirements some months in advance, which are then the subject of product call downs as and when required, the size and regularity of such call downs will help set deadlines for any mitigation strategy after an insured incident. In the case of orders for very major items, such as multiple aeroplane engines, the delivery schedules may involve very lengthy periods between deliveries. For other assets, weekly or more frequent deliveries might be required. In any case, and after considering the availability of buffer stock, the necessary length of the Maximum Indemnity Period can be assessed.

These principles also apply where a product is supplied on a just in time basis. Buffer stocks are likely to be minimal and the risk of any shortfall in production translating into a loss of profit significantly increased.

Basis of Sales

To understand the impact of an incident on a business, loss adjusters will typically enquire as to whether sales are effected on the basis of price or quality (the latter representing the level of service for a non-manufacturing business). A price driven business will find it easier to mitigate an insured event occurring, whereas a business selling a product which it has held out to be 'better' than that of a competitor is going to find it more difficult. Luxury cars (or any expensive product to some extent) will not be sold unless the sales environment and ambience is correct. Even non-visible damage will produce a difficulty - water ingress at the rear of the premises affecting carpets etc. is likely to generate a smell which may produce a disinclination to purchase unless addressed rapidly.

Subcontracting for a manufacturing business selling on the basis of quality will be more difficult as competitors will by definition be perceived to have inferior quality standards to those of the insured business itself. Where the staff of the insured business are working on machine capacity rented from another business on a night shift, for example, senior management may have to be based at those premises to ensure that any defect or shortfall in quality is identified at the earliest possible time. The cost of rectifying defects subsequently will always be more significant than the additional time cost of establishing thorough quality control procedures.

It has previously been noted that the additional pressures that such an arrangement can bring to relatively few key individuals (particularly when their skills will be in more demand at the Premises themselves than ever before) can be very significant. An over reliance on a few individuals, which may be an unavoidable reality in many businesses, represents a special risk in the event of a claim.

Two final observations should be made with regard to how sales are achieved, and the role of advertising:

Firstly, a manufacturing business which sells its products via sales representatives visiting customers will be more able to mitigate an incident occurring at the Premises than a business generating income from customers visiting site. Extensive Damage may appear to be particularly bad but may not hamper production as much as a (less visually obvious) breakdown in a critical machine.

Customers, however, are likely to react more adversely to the former than the latter. If they do not visit the Premises, and supply can be maintained, there is less chance of an overreaction to apparently severe but not critical damage. Where sales are achieved at the Premises, as is the case with retailers and car showrooms, for example, it is less easy to move the focus away from obvious damage via uninterrupted service.

In between these two extremes are professional businesses such as firms of accountants and solicitors, who will visit many clients off site but who will also rely on prestigious offices for those clients or prospects who visit.

The experience of claims confirms the truism that if sales are achieved either by sales representatives off site, over the telephone, or over the Internet, rather than to visitors physically attending the premises then the opportunity to effectively mitigate a loss through the expenditure of increased costs will be significant.

Businesses selling to customers visiting the Premises are likely to suffer longer from an incident involving obvious damage and are likely to need the protection of longer indemnity periods.

Of course, competitors will learn about the incident and will bring it to the attention of as many customers as possible. In some cases, even where customers do not attend the premises and might otherwise not know about an incident, it might be advisable to manage any gossip by confirming that something has occurred. A positive communication, to customers or in the trade press set in the context of an established mitigation strategy, can be issued. If alternative processes have been established such that no interruption in supply will occur, gossip from competitors is likely to be counter productive for them.

Secondly, with regard to advertising, there are three observations to offer:

1) It is possible to over advertise after an insured event, thereby creating customer demand which cannot be met through reduced productive capacity post incident. This compounds the disappointment of customers created by earlier service failures after the insured event and is likely to exacerbate business interruption losses arising. A business which relies heavily on advertising as a matter of routine is more likely to risk raising customer expectations for a sales promotion or new range of products, which if not met will produce greater levels of gross profit and a greater period of time required to recover from the incident.

2) Where advertising has taken place and an insured event prevents sales being effected in the normal manner, it is not uncommon for businesses to claim the cost of the (wasted) advertising from insurers. Given that such advertising took place pre incident, these costs cannot be dealt with as an Increased Cost of Working. This is a further example of wasted costs, and a loss which is a consequence of an insured incident but not one which will be covered by insurers. Of course, if it could be demonstrated that such advertising would have supported increased

Turnover (or maintained existing Turnover) after the incident then by definition the insured business would be indemnified for that within calculation of the Reduction in Turnover and the loss of Gross Profit thereon.

3) There are businesses that historically have never advertised and these include high quality businesses such as restaurants that may have relied previously on word of mouth and a good reputation to attract business. Following a major incident, a business which trades on the basis of reputation is likely to find it more difficult to recover and will need to consider advertising to re-establish turnover to its pre incident level, even if this has not been undertaken before.

Contractual Penalties

In some cases, businesses are bound to make liquidated penalty payments to customers in the case of non performance. Such contractual penalties will primarily be incurred because of an historic contractual commitment (written or oral) and not solely to avoid a reduction in turnover in the future. These may not be dealt with as Increased Costs, therefore, and if it is desirable to cover these under an insurance policy, then a separate Fines and Penalties extension (discussed in chapter 6) may be required. To avoid any misunderstandings, underwriters' views as to whether penalties fall within the scope of the cover or not could be established in advance of any claim being made.

In some cases, contractual penalties may be expressly excluded from the cover, which removes any uncertainty about the matter.

Capacity Issues

Issues connected with capacity and the availability thereof to mitigate business interruption losses arising are a very common cause of difficulty.

In the case of manufacturing businesses it may be advised that not all of the plant is working on a twenty-four-hour, seven day per week basis, but that key machines through which all production passes are. It may, therefore, be suggested that there is no available capacity to increase production or work additional overtime following an incident. It would be unusual for such a business to have drawn this feature out for the benefit of insurers at inception/renewal and insurers may only learn that a loss of production will be directly translated into a loss of gross profit if a claim is made. A fundamental restriction on the ability to mitigate a loss can potentially be significant enough to constitute a non disclosure issue which would speak to the foundation of the policy. To avoid the difficulty the claim will bring, therefore, the disclosure of this matter at inception/renewal is advisable.

Machine hours are not the only constraint. There may be a disinclination on the part of employees to work overtime. This may be the case where, for example, a significant part of the business represents shift workers for whom it is convenient to work the particular shift undertaken, but who may be disinclined or simply unable to work other hours. Whilst less of an issue than was the case historically, heavy unionised businesses can also suffer a reduction in flexibility.

The issue of restricted capacity to mitigate does not only relate to manufacturing businesses. Accountants and solicitors may argue that they cannot work overtime as all staff are working to the best of their ability and for all available hours already. In the case of departments in such businesses where a sufficient degree of desktop work is undertaken, it might be the case that the service provided is in effect a commoditised product. It could be suggested that the expectation that professionals will work additional hours for the good of the firm might not reflect the reality.

There are other businesses whose assertions that additional hours cannot be worked are less easy to accept. Dental practices operating 9-5, five days per week, for example, can invariably open on a Saturday morning post loss, even if this is not usual, particularly given the existence of a number of patients who would appreciate an appointment outside the working day. A disinclination to arrange such Saturday working would not be reason enough for Gross Profit/Gross Revenue losses to be paid. The release of funds equivalent to the increased costs that would be incurred in such extended working would be a compromise - alternatively, an insurer might consider an unwillingness to mitigate a loss more seriously.

The issue here is not to question whether a restriction on mitigating a loss is real or imagined, but merely to ensure that the clarity and volume with which mitigation difficulties and limitations are identified at claims time is mirrored at inception/renewal.

Related Party Transactions

Consider the following historic circumstance:

> *A husband and wife, trading as a partnership, manufacture ammunition boxes, selling them to husband trading separately as a sole proprietor. Husband stocks them and sells them on to the end customer. An insurance policy is arranged covering the partnership only.*
>
> *There is a fire in the ammunition box making machine, such that the partnership cannot sell boxes to husband for around nine months. The latter has so much stock that he is able to supply the end customer without interruption.*

As to whether the above loss is covered, there are four potential answers:

1) The policy has been issued in the name of the partnership without reference to the husband and the reduction in turnover suffered by that partnership should, therefore, be dealt with in full by insurers. This conclusion implies an onus in establishing risk on insurers, who may have not asked any questions about the business or customer base at inception.

2) The fact that all of the turnover is achieved by the husband (and wife as business partner) selling to himself represents a material non disclosure - the policy should be avoided ab initio and no payment made. This conclusion places an onus on the insured business to disclose material issues whether explicitly questioned by insurers at inception or not.

3) In reality, the husband's stock holding business and the manufacturing activity undertaken by the partnership constitute one business and insurers should pay for the additional cost in reconstituting the buffer stock used by the husband under the auspices of the Accumulated Stocks Clause.

4) No loss has been suffered. The husband was massively overstocking ammunition boxes and the business has realised the optimum level as a consequence of the incident.

In fact, whilst this matter was being formally considered, the husband indicated that he did not wish to pursue the claim, he was divorcing his wife at the time and preferred to receive nothing from insurers rather than have to give her half. Notwithstanding that, the case raised an interesting issue. No generic answer is offered - the particular merits of any circumstance would need to be considered.

Where a business is selling products or purchasing products from another business over which it exerts control, then it is obviously in a position to dictate the price charged both before and after an incident. Where such a business is inclined to do so, increased loss covered by the policy could be artificially created. Selling prices to a related business could be depressed post incident resulting in savings for that other business as well as a greater payment from insurers through an increased reduction in turnover on the part of the business suffering the incident.

It is not suggested that dishonesty will necessarily arise. In many cases, the fact that the customer/supplier is a related business will actually increase flexibility post incident and help to mitigate a loss. The point, however, is that the existence of such a related party should be disclosed to avoid difficulty subsequently.

There is a similar situation in terms of renting premises from family businesses, particularly where these constitute alternative premises post incident and give rise to a claim for increased costs. This is not in itself a difficulty. The problem that related party transactions present is that they may be at a higher or lower level than the third party arms length rate.

As long as they are set at the same level and set on the same basis that would be the case with unrelated third parties, they need not represent a difficulty at all. The issue of disclosure at renewal or inception merely avoids the perception that this might not be the case.

Another example of a related party transaction arose as follows:

> *'The insured business was a major electricity generating company that elected to construct a new power station. In so doing, a separate limited company was incorporated through whose books all of the costs were passed. The business insured that separate limited company under an Advanced Profits cover. The Advanced Profits policy covered the recharge of costs incurred in building the power station over a twenty year period back to the electricity generating plc. An insured event delayed commission of the power station and the subsequent recharge of costs back to the plc.'*

The above situation can be summarised diagrammatically:

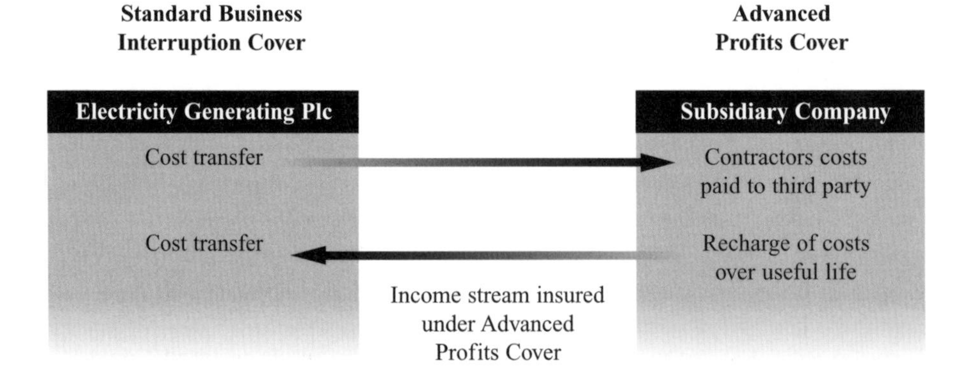

The plc reasonably wished to write-off the costs of building a power station over the period of time that it would generate power. To achieve this, a separate (wholly owned) subsidiary company was established which was the vehicle for what were, in effect, book entries recording costs incurred. By insuring the subsidiary only, insurers had inadvertently exposed themselves to making cash payments for these book entries (i.e. by funding the delayed cost recharge) between one part of a group of businesses and another. (The problem would not have arisen if all of these businesses had been insured under a group policy. It is accepted that an advanced profits cover for the group may have entailed a greater payment by insurers which would recognise the delay in charging profit as well as covering costs to external customers.)

In the particular case referred to, given that the insurers knew the identity of the entities involved, a payment was made under the policy. Significant delay accrued whilst the formal aspects were considered prior to such a payment being made.

Alteration of Risk

The alteration of risk condition often (though not always) relates to the material damage cover rather than the business interruption. Generally speaking, therefore, an alteration of risk affecting the business interruption aspect only would not require disclosure part way through a policy period, albeit there would still be a duty to disclose at renewal.

The notable exception to this is the circumstance where a business goes into receivership or administration, which must be notified immediately. The existing policy cover ceases. A separate policy can then be taken out to cover the new risks presenting themselves. There are various schemes run by national brokers that provide such cover. (A claim would not be invalidated by the insolvency if it occurred prior to that commencing. It could still be dealt with on its merits.)

If an insured incident causes delay in completion of a contract for a customer, generally speaking, overtime working can be undertaken to try and rectify the situation and the increased cost claim will relate to the overtime only. In the case of a Receivership, the Receiver may have drawn up a programme of redundancies which will have to be forestalled if staff have to be kept on to complete contracts. The additional cost would then comprise the whole of the salary costs of those individuals retained beyond the redundancy date but for the incident, resulting in a significantly higher increased cost.

In-house Development

The issue of using in-house staff to develop production plant, IT work stations and other equipment has already been raised. In some cases, the assets designed in-house will directly generate sales. The jewellery salesman who suffers the theft of his samples was previously cited as an example. In other cases, the assets will support the business development more generally.

Consider the following :

An insured business produces state of the art technology in the automotive industry, and, rather than demonstrate their product via computer simulation, invites customers to actually drive vehicles fitted with the technology to experience it first-hand. Following a significant loss, affecting the buildings and contents generally, the sole vehicle fitted with a particular technology was written-off and there was an inability for customers to appreciate the technology other than via computer simulation. Interest from customers dropped off. As a result, a significant Gross Profit loss was claimed. The insured business had not drawn the insurer's attention to the importance of the demonstration vehicle prior to the loss.

The insured business in this particular instance was able to show that the demonstration vehicle had been booked on to an aeroplane to be taken to North America for demonstration to a vehicle manufacturer prior to the insured incident. The demonstration would have taken place around two weeks thereafter but for the Damage. This was undisputed. The issue centred around the ability of the insured business to demonstrate whether or not the customer would have commissioned further research, producing a revenue stream within the Maximum Indemnity Period.

Because the technology was innovative, there was no track record of similar demonstrations that could be drawn upon and no separate contingency cover had been arranged. In the final analysis the insured business was unable to demonstrate that revenue had been lost as a consequence of the Damage. It was also considered relevant that the technology (which had initially been developed over a significant period of time) could not easily be replicated post incident, which challenged the ultimate success of the product even if customers had been keen to invest.

Where there can be difficulties in quantifying loss, a failure to properly discuss the issue pre claim is only likely to exacerbate difficulties. Had the matter been discussed and raised, a separate contingency cover might have been arranged within agreed parameters, and protocols for investigation and quantification of loss agreed, insurers appreciating and being prepared to take the risk in return for the appropriate premium.

5. Cornerstones of Cover

There are two areas fundamental to the business interruption cover.

The first is the **calculation of Gross Profit** (and the assumption that a Gross Profit policy is appropriate as opposed to a Gross Revenue policy).

The second is the **selection of the Maximum Indemnity Period**

Calculation of Gross Profit

Gross Revenue/Gross Profit

Policies are written on a Gross Revenue or Gross Turnover basis (or on the basis of sales or takings or some similar term) for businesses that do not make significant tangible physical purchases and for whom the term Gross Profit may be anachronistic. These include firms of professionals, consulting engineers or hotels. The policy is being written on a basis most meaningful to the insured business. The indemnity provided, given that both the Gross Profit and the Gross Revenue policy seek to provide an indemnity, should in theory be the same.

Gross Profit is specifically defined in each policy wording. An insured business selects which costs to deduct from turnover to define gross profit in the most relevant way for that business. Typically, these would comprise purchases (net of discounts received), carriage inwards and bad debts. The definition selected may differ from that used in the annual accounts. The latter may include some deduction for staff wages, for example. There is consequentially a potential danger of under declaration if an accounts gross profit figure is imported unquestioned into the insurance cover.

Consider the following example to illustrate the point:

J Bloggs & Co suffer a loss of turnover amounting to £40,000 in spring 2005. The most recent accounts to 31 December 2004 show the following:

	£'000	***£'000***
Turnover		*100*
Opening Stock	*5*	
Add purchases	*25*	
Add power costs	*10*	
Less closing stock	*(5)*	
Cost of sales		*(35)*
Gross Profit		*65*
Fixed costs	*35*	
Variable costs	*15*	
Total overheads		*(50)*
Net profit		*15*

Assuming that there are no increased costs to deal with and assuming that savings amount to £10,000, what are the amounts payable on Gross Revenue and Gross Profit basis?

The operation of the policy cover was set out previously. For a Gross Profit policy, the Rate of Gross Profit from the accounts is 65% (£65,000 as a percentage of £100,000). However, power costs would generally not be deducted from turnover in calculating Gross Profit for insurance purposes. The profit for insurance purposes would, therefore, be £75,000 giving an effective Rate of Gross Profit of 75%. The loss of Gross Profit would amount to £30,000 (£40,000 lost turnover at 75%) from which savings of £10,000 would be deducted to give a settlement of £20,000.

As far as Gross Revenue cover is concerned, it would be an easy mistake to make to assume that the calculation is simply £40,000 lost turnover, less £10,000 savings to give a settlement of £30,000.

This overlooks the fact that a Gross Profit policy deducts costs from turnover in two stages. Firstly, there is the deduction of costs to arrive at the Rate of Gross Profit which the insured business **assumed** would decline proportionately with turnover. Reduced (purchase) costs of £10,000 were, therefore, deducted from turnover to arrive at the initial Gross Profit loss of £30,000. The Gross Profit policy then deducted a further £10,000 (Savings, as defined in the policy) relating to the **actual** (not the assumed) reduction in costs subsequent to the incident.

The Gross Revenue policy does not require the deduction of **assumed** costs. Only those costs that do actually reduce are taken off the loss of turnover in calculating a settlement. In respect of the hypothetical example above, from the loss of revenue of £40,000 it is necessary to deduct the £10,000 relating to the reduction in purchase costs, and then the £10,000 savings. In other words £20,000 will be deducted to provide the same settlement as the Gross Profit cover.

There is an assumption herein, of course, and that is that the purchase costs (or any other costs which are uninsured) will decline proportionately with turnover exactly as assumed. For reasons discussed more fully below, purchase costs may not, in fact, decline proportionately with turnover. The assumed level of reduction would still be applied to the Gross Profit policy, but the Gross Revenue policy would only reflect the extent to which costs actually did go down.

It follows that the risk of assumption, i.e. in guessing which costs will decline proportionately with turnover, lies with the insured person in respect of a Gross Profit policy. The risk of assumption for a Gross Revenue policy lies with the underwriter, who will have to make an assumption about the extent to which costs will reduce after an insured incident in carrying out his Estimated Maximum Loss calculations. For this reason, a Gross Revenue policy is superior as far as the insured person is concerned albeit the premium that an underwriter would charge would reflect that.

Of course, there is little point in paying a premium to insure a cost that will definitely reduce proportionately of turnover. The difficulty lies in being sure which costs will behave in that way. The unequivocal experience of claims is that costs do not reduce proportionately with turnover. There should be a presumption that costs will not be deducted from turnover in calculating Gross Profit unless it is a certainty that they will reduce in-line with turnover regardless of the circumstance. Contrast this with the situation where certain costs are deducted from turnover as a matter of course without careful consideration of whether such an approach has merit.

Costs other than Purchases

Many policies deduct from turnover (i.e. uninsure) bad debts and carriage costs as a matter of course. Some proportion of power costs and employee wages may also be deducted.

In the hypothetical example set out above, power costs were deducted in calculating Gross Profit for accounts purposes. It is not uncommon (albeit often inappropriate) for a business to establish its Gross Profit sum insured with reference to its accounting profit and in the hypothetical example, the Rate of Gross Profit will be 65% not 75%. The Loss of Gross Profit payable would then have been not £30,000 but £26,000. Were it to be the case that power costs did not reduce proportionately with turnover (and experience suggests that such costs do not decline as envisaged) then a shortfall of £4,000 would be suffered on settlement of the claim.

The fact that costs might have been uninsured either inadvertently or without a proper appreciation of how this would impact upon any settlement is irrelevant. The danger of inadvertency can be avoided by assuming that Revenue is the correct starting point for establishing the insurable amount. Subsequently, only the costs that will substantively and definitely decline inline with turnover, regardless of the circumstances of any event, after proper consideration each year, should be deducted. This avoids the possibility of error that can arise if the Gross Profit in the annual accounts is the starting point.

In theory, the concept that power should reduce, for example, or that carriage costs in delivering product to customers should reduce proportionately with turnover is understandable.

However, 90% of incidents represent partial losses rather than complete disasters, and some hindrance to production is far more likely than a cessation thereof. A machine is more likely to be powered-up and running but not operating as efficiently, or producing the same quantity of product as before rather than completely destroyed. The quantity of goods produced would diminish and with it turnover unless extended overtime working at additional cost could be arranged.

The additional costs relating to power in working overtime would still be dealt with as part of the claim. However, if power costs were named as an Uninsured Working Expense, there would be a deduction in arriving at the

Gross Profit payment due, to reflect the assumption that power costs would go down regardless of the fact that this assumption could subsequently prove to be wrong.

The same can occur with carriage costs. The likelihood is for a partial loss to occur as opposed to complete devastation. Reduced efficiency and depressed throughput may cause the three-piece suite manufacturer, for example, to despatch sofas individually as soon as they are ready rather than delivering half a dozen on a lorry at the same time. Whilst the additional cost over and above normal carriage costs would be dealt with as an increased cost, there would again be a deduction to reflect the assumption that the normal element of carriage costs would reduce, notwithstanding the fact that the assumption was subsequently demonstrated to be wrong.

The reduction in premium resulting from the deduction of such costs as power, or even proportions thereof, is not normally significant enough to justify the risk of assumption being accepted.

The most significant cost, other than purchases, which tends to be uninsured relates to wages. The days when staff could be turned away from the factory gate as being superfluous to that particular day's production are long gone. Setting aside casual staff, the standing labour cost for most businesses now represents a fixed rather than a variable cost. It would be an unusual business that would wish to make the workforce redundant after an insured event and the cost should, therefore, be insured (i.e. not deducted from turnover in calculating Gross Profit). Even were this the intent, redundancy costs can typically represent three to six months of the normal salary cost and the amount of the reduction in costs that might be derived from wholesale redundancy even after a disaster would, therefore, represent very significantly less than a full year's expense.

The tendency to uninsure wages derives from the expectation of disaster rather than partial loss. The partial loss is more likely, depressed efficiency typically leading to the need for extended rather than reduced hours. In the retail sector, Gross Profit might be calculated on the basis that, if a shop is burnt down, there will be savings in staff costs, power, and all operational costs. However, the more likely event is that there will be an escape of water or some other event which tarnishes the ambience of the shop. The staff may, therefore, be present and the lights on, but customers may not linger and may not choose to buy. The partial loss again presents itself. Turnover will reduce, but the costs may not.

Of course, the doomsday approach, which assumes catastrophy, would be entirely appropriate if the insured business explicitly only intends to cover such situations. What is far more common is for there to be an intention for the policy to respond to all but insignificant incidences rather than disasters, and those costs which are uninsured ought to be selected on that basis.

The cost of casual staff, where they are unskilled, their emotional intelligence unimportant, and a buoyant local labour market able to easily supply replacements, might be uninsured. Even with all of these circumstances satisfied, the period of downtime would still need to be long enough to bear the redundancy costs (and negative local press comment) and still show cost savings. Night workers in petrol stations might fall into this category as might shelf stackers at supermarkets. Bar staff, however, are required to have emotional intelligence and the value of charismatic bar staff is generally appreciated.

In the case of some employees, the concern will be to properly involve them in the post incident response plan to retain them rather than there being any question of them being made redundant.

Chefs at restaurants are an excellent example. Any decent chef is going to want to carry on creating menus and experimenting with cookery notwithstanding that the restaurant and/or hotel may have burnt down. It is not uncommon to have to arrange temporary portable kitchens to allow chefs to undertake their creative activity even though the food produced may simply be disposed of at the end of the day.

A better alternative is to transfer valued staff to other premises where these are available or even to consider loaning them to another business on an agreed basis. (This does court the danger that a chef may not return. Of course, if nothing is done it is highly likely that a good chef will leave and will then definitely not return.) The occurrence of an insured event requires normally unpalatable courses of action to be considered. Effective mitigation plans require the least worst options to be identified.

Some businesses hire workers on hourly rates to carry out unskilled work as and when business is secured from customers. In such a case, the assumption that wage costs will decline proportionately with turnover may have more merit but the general market experience is that wage costs, as with power and other expense categories will not reduce in proportion with turnover, albeit some level of reduction may arise.

Having suggested that costs should not be uninsured, it must be observed that, if a claim is made, those costs that do decline proportionately with turnover will be deducted prior to calculation of settlement as savings. With hindsight, an insured business might be critical of the fact that it was encouraged to pay premium in respect of an expense category, but derived no benefit from so doing (the relevant expense having been deducted as a saving). The answer is that each set of circumstances represents an unforeseen event, and the fact that on one occasion a cost might decline to a greater extent that on another, does not justify courting the risk of assuming that significant cost reductions will always materialise.

Purchases

It is commonly taken for granted that purchases will decline proportionately with turnover and in many instances this will be the case. Consider a business providing airtime to telephony users that buys capacity itself only as customers require it, generating a profit from the markup on purchased time as and when that airtime is required. In such a situation those costs might be uninsured.

In the waste industry, by way of contrast, the processor may be paid to take in raw material that will subsequently be made into something new. Such a business enjoys a purchase income rather than cost. If processing is halted by an incident, it might be necessary to pay for part processed materials as well as penalties arising for not receiving volumes of waste contractually committed to with suppliers.

A universally relevant approach cannot be assumed. For insurance companies, rather than insuring Gross Revenue, on average (subject to exposure to significant risks) it might be reasonable to assume that claims will vary proportionately with turnover and might also be uninsured. It is not the intention to suggest that purchases will not decline, but more that the assumption that they will decline ought to be properly validated.

Consider the following circumstance:

A business purchases eggs and uses an advanced piece of plant (the cracking machine) to split the egg yolks and whites for processing by different departments for different groups of customers thus:

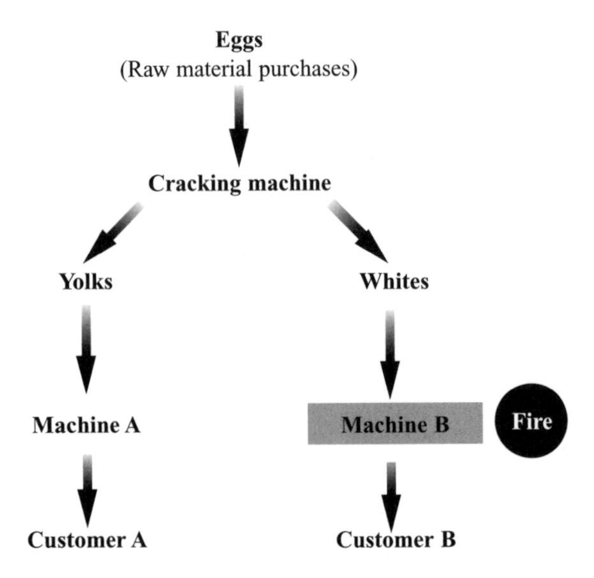

Given that this was a manufacturing business, a Gross Profit policy was established on the basis that if turnover was lost eggs would not have to be bought. In fact, there was a fire on one of the key machines in Machine Group B, resulting in an inability to process egg whites for Pavlovas, Roulades, et al. It transpired that, in order to obtain the egg yolks (that line was still operational), it was still necessary to buy the egg. Purchases did not, therefore, decline at all but the Rate of Gross Profit applied to the Reduction in Turnover reflected the assumption that the expense would. A very substantial shortfall arose when comparing the settlement with the actual losses incurred.

Four other examples will also be offered to challenge the assumption that Purchases should be uninsured.

1. Contractual Commitments

There are many businesses that have contracted forward to purchase raw material regardless of the subsequent operation of an insured event.

Consider the following circumstance:

A business was engaged in the dehydration of vegetables. Each year suppliers would be contracted to grow particular crops which would then be passed along a dehydration line, bagged up, and sold off in small lots until the following harvest was due. A fire occurred on the dehydration line shortly before a crop was due to be received and this could consequently not be taken in. The insured business had uninsured the purchase expense but the crops still had to be bought, as contractually required.

Consideration was given to storing the product in deep freeze until repairs were completed. The very significant cost of holding various vegetable crops in deep freeze, not just until the machine was repaired, but until the dehydration backlog had been dealt with, rendered the expense highly uneconomic. Additional Increased Cost of Working cover would have been required to alter the situation.

The same situation is true of crisp manufacturers who will require a certain sort of potato and will contract forward to purchase it. In fact, many food producers will do this with a range of raw materials and this fundamentally challenges the assumption that purchases will reduce.

Finance directors may suggest that the product is a commodity which can be sold on if there is some difficulty in processing it in-house. That again is mere assumption. For the business to suffer a significant incident, a combination of circumstances would have to arise. There would perhaps be a surplus crop of that particular product at the relevant time which meant that, whilst some proceeds would be achieved, a very significant shortfall would still accrue. Whilst in normal circumstances, therefore, selling the product on might resolve the issue, a combination of unforeseen circumstances could mean that would simply not be possible.

2. Commercial Commitments

The above discussion relates to businesses contractually required to make Purchases regardless of Damage. There are other firms that may not be contractually required to make a purchase, but may be commercially required to do so. The variety of such businesses is significant.

Consider the case of a scrap metal merchant. It may take many years to develop a good scrap round. If the business suffers a fire affecting the fragmentiser at the Premises, no scrap will be processed. Suppliers, of course, will continue to produce scrap as a by-product of their own manufacturing activity on a daily basis, and, regardless of goodwill feelings toward the insured business, will still require it to be removed. If other scrap merchants are given the opportunity to step in and help out, it might well be that the customers will stay with those alternative suppliers, such that no raw materials are available when the fragmentiser is repaired. The business might not survive after the end of the Maximum Indemnity Period when the support of the insurance policy expires.

Commercially, the scrap metal merchant may have to carry on collecting scrap (at least from those customers producing scrap of a good quality) and very significant shortfalls (settlement proceeds compared to actual loss arising) can arise if the Purchases have to continue, but have been uninsured.

To a lesser extent it can also be seen in the printing industry where unusual types of paper are required. Following insured incidents in the past, it has become apparent that certain types of specialist paper may not be readily available to allow replenishment of stocks. Substantial printing businesses providing a lot of turnover to paper suppliers are able to exercise commercial muscle and obtain what they require. If such printing businesses suffer an insured event and do not provide the paper supplier with the levels of throughput that previously underpinned the relationship, then it can become difficult to obtain supplies and not only higher prices, but also significant delays might arise in securing product elsewhere. Whilst such additional costs will be dealt with by a standard policy wording were that to be necessary, such a business might prefer (at least in the short-term) to carry on making Purchases to some extent to secure the particular supply avenue. It might still be appropriate to uninsure Purchases generally, but it will be helpful for the insured business to understand in advance of any claim that, if it continues to make such Purchases in specific circumstances, they will not be paid by the insurer.

3. Stepped Discounts

Purchases are normally defined in policies as being net of discounts received. Even where the policy provides no such definition, a claim would be settled with reference to the categorisation normally used in the annual accounts (the Accounts Designation Clause), which will almost always relate to purchases net of discounts received.

There are businesses whose Purchase costs benefit from aggressive stepped discounts. If a business buys 100 widgets for £1 say, it may receive a 10% bulk discount. Its normal annual Purchase cost will, therefore, be £90. Following an insured event, it may only buy 95 widgets, thereby losing its eligibility for the 10% discount. The Purchase cost post incident of £95 is higher than that normally incurred (£90), but the consequential loss of £5 would not be one covered by the policy, assuming that Purchases have been uninsured.

The issue of discounts is not relevant where there is a standard discount percentage applied to all purchases - the number of widgets purchased would not alter the proportion of discount achieved. Where there are stepped discounts, however, as can still be the case for car dealers, or for importers of new technology (games consoles, for example, at launch time), then there could be a modest Revenue loss which results in Purchase discounts being missed and a subsequent significant reduction in Gross Profit. A lost vehicle sale of say £15,000 might cause a bonus threshold offering £50,000 being missed. A loss of profit significantly higher than the Revenue loss might ensue. That loss of Gross Profit would arise from an increase in costs that was uninsured rather than from a reduction in turnover and would not be covered by the policy.

4. Departmental Variation

There are businesses with strong departmental variations. Car garages may engage in second-hand and new car sales, repair/service and MOT work. Margins on the sale of both second-hand and new vehicles would differ, whilst both being significantly lower than the insurance Rate of Gross Profit for MOT business, which will be 100% (assuming that wages were not uninsured).

Similarly, in hotels, Revenue generated through affiliated leisure facilities as well as that relating to room accommodation would likely to be approaching a 100% Rate of Gross Profit for insurance purposes. Margins enjoyed in the restaurant or bar would be more modest.

One interesting claim highlighted this issue with regards to holiday camps. A policy for a large single site chalet based camp, which featured an entertainment centre and shopping complex on-site, had been established on a Gross Profit basis. A number of chalets on the holiday site burnt down and a loss of revenue resulted.

The insured business sought to claim for a pure loss of Revenue (100% Gross Profit), i.e. the rent that the damaged chalet would have generated, notwithstanding that the policy assumed (at the option of the insured business) that Purchase costs would reduce proportionately with turnover. In that particular case, it was difficult to substantiate a corresponding loss of turnover at the site shops and facilities - the number of damaged chalets was not so great as to produce a large enough turnover variance to be identifiable by trend analysis. The matter was ultimately settled to the satisfaction of all concerned but the inappropriateness of assuming a uniform level of profit across all parts of the business was noted by the insured business.

The Departmental Clause is considered elsewhere, and does allow for separate rates of Gross Profit to be claimed where the results of the business are separately identifiable, but makes no such allowance where they are not. The holiday site claim was eventually resolved but not without complication - the all-inclusive price paid by guests included use of many of the amenities, meals in the restaurant etc. The overall profit proved to be difficult to attribute to the different parts of the business.

Care should be taken in uninsuring Purchases when different departments of the business enjoy significantly different rates of gross profit - the ability of the insured business to evidence different rates should be considered before assuming that the Departmental clause will be of assistance if a claim is made. If the differing rates cannot be separately established, then Purchases should potentially be insured, the policy being written on a Gross Revenue basis.

Manufacturing businesses may have different departments which all contribute value to the end product but which are not separate profit centres. The presumption that Purchases constitute the same proportion of turnover in each part of the business and will uniformly decrease proportionately with turnover has been demonstrated to be wrong on many occasions.

Uninsuring Costs - Conclusions and Example Rates

Annual reconsideration of each uninsured expense will help avoid any misunderstandings about what assumptions were made, who made them, and how any claim settlement would be altered by those assumptions. Importantly, it will help to emphasise the point to the purchaser of insurance that the definition of Gross Profit used in the accounts will not necessarily represent the most sensible basis to be used for an insurance policy.

It is not unusual for finance directors to refer to the difference between the insurance and accounts basis in a critical manner as if the insurance approach adds unnecessary complication. This is partly a fault of the insurance industry in failing to present the policy mechanism as a virtue rather than a vice. Insurers are providing the flexibility to the insured businesses to select, without being bound by an accounts definition or any other factor, those costs that they, with their intimate knowledge of their business, believe will reduce, to provide a policy most meaningful for them.

The fact that none of the Companies Acts (or other piece of Statute) define gross profit, or that accounting and financial standards allow businesses to define gross profit on the basis most meaningful to their particular operation, represents necessary and welcome flexibility. The lack of any standard legal or commercial definition of gross profit can consequently make a finance director perceive the insurance approach to be unduly restrictive and a failure to engage with the underlying principles at inception/renewal is a common cause of difficulty when the claim is made. Problems tend to arise not due to the fault of the insurer or the broker, but of the insured entity, which may have provided insufficient information and/or time to explain their business properly in advance and to allow the policy to be written on an optimal basis.

It may be of assistance to set out some typical gross profit rates as they pertain to insurance policies as a reference point, albeit with the proviso that each business is different and has the capacity to deviate from the norm:

Nature of Business	Average % Rate of Gross Profit
Audio/Visual Retailer/Repairers	.30
Bakery	.57
Butcher	.33
Café	.58
Care Home	.69
Circuit Board Manufacturers	.63
Clothing Designers/Importers	.25
Coach Builders	.43
Coloured Dye Suppliers	.59
Cosmetics Manufacturers	.74
Dentist	.85
Dry Cleaners/Launderette	.75
Electrical Contractors	.50
Electro-Platers	.67
Embroiderers	.50
Engineering Machinists	.83
Floor Covering Wholesaler	.34
Furrier	.60
Garden Center	.50
Hair & Beauty Salon	.70
Hoteliers	.67
Industrial Paint Manufacturers	.41
Joiners	.71
Lighting Manufacturers	.59
Manufacture - Carpets	.46
Manufacture - Electrical Appliances	.54
Manufacture - Furniture	.51
Manufacture - Lead Crystal	.48
Manufacture - Motor Components	.42
Manufacture of Electronic Goods	.47
Manufacture of Garden Sheds	.53
Manufacture of Plastic Goods	.53
Metal Fabricators	.46
Metal Manufacturers	.27
Motor Vehicle Repairs	.64
Newsagent	.24
Opticians	.63
Petrol Station	.25
Picture Frame Retailers	.54

Nature of Business	Average % Rate of Gross Profit
Poultry Processing	48
Printers	70
Public House	55
Restaurant	62
Retail - Catering	78
Retail - Ceramic Tiles	12
Retail - Toys	43
Retail - Clothing	50
Retail - Cosmetics	45
Retail - Electrical Goods	42
Retail - Fireplaces	55
Retail - Floor Covering	56
Retail - Furniture	49
Retail - General	51
Retail - Greeting Cards	60
Retail - Grocery Store	20
Retail - Jewellers	40
Retail - Mobile Phone	33
Retail - Musical Instruments	31
Retail - Pet Shop	45
Retail - Shoes	45
Retail - Sportswear/Equipment	44
Retail - Stationery	35
Sports Club	95
Steel Fabricators	34
Suppliers of Fish & Equipment	40
Suppliers of Material Handling Equipment	24
Takeaway - Fish & Chip Shop	56
Takeaway - Indian	68
Takeaway Fast Food	42
Tattoo & Body Piercing Salon	66
Timber Merchants	26
Tool Hire	82
Used Car Sales	26
Video Rental Shop	85

Source: Analysis of Cunningham Lindsey UK's business interruption claims over a four-year-period.

The above rates are provided for guidance only, providing a yard stick against which to compare rates proposed by the accounts department of an insured business. A significant difference to the above would not suggest that the proposed rate is incorrect, merely that a double-check might be appropriate. The rates typically assume that purchases, carriage and bad debts (only) are uninsured, albeit the precise policy definitions supporting them vary. Rates of Gross Profit according to annual accounts might be significantly lower than the above, if they are stated after deduction for wages, power etc.

Indemnity Period Selection

The indemnity period is defined in the Association of British Insurers' (ABI) standard wording as follows:

"The period beginning with the occurrence of the Damage and ending not later than the Maximum Indemnity Period thereafter during which the results of the Business shall be affected in consequence of the Damage."

The wording does not require the results of the business to be depressed, but merely different from what they would have been had there not been an insured event. This can involve increased or decreased turnover, and/or higher or lower costs being incurred.

On one occasion a hostel providing bed and breakfast accommodation to DSS claimants suffered extensive smoke Damage requiring redecoration and refurbishment throughout.

Following the completion of repairs the premises reopened as a hotel charging approximately double the room rate that previously applied. Not only was the room rate higher, but the occupancy rate was also significantly higher such that the additional income gained through operating as a hotel after refurbishment more than made up for the loss arising during the initial period of closure. Quite correctly, no Gross Profit (or, as appropriate, Gross Revenue) losses were payable as a consequence. The insured business sought to argue that they should be allowed to claim for their losses incurred during the initial period of closure, unilaterally ending the indemnity period when those losses ceased. That would be appropriate if the indemnity period was defined as the period during which the results were depressed, but that is not what policy wordings say.

Likewise, there may be no impact on gross profit on an ongoing basis but increased costs might be incurred and the indemnity period would continue until the point at which such increased costs were curtailed. The ongoing increased costs continue to affect the results of the business in the interim.

The actual indemnity period is different to the Maximum Indemnity Period, which is the point after which insurers will no longer pay for losses even if they continue.

It is obviously important to ensure that an appropriately long Maximum Indemnity Period is selected prior to any claim.

Just over **75%** of policies have a twelve-month Maximum Indemnity Period. It is suggested that **twelve-months is likely to be too short a period** in many cases. It is sensible to assume significant Damage will give rise to a significant rebuild time. Assuming that the building is the longest lead time item (i.e. contents, plant and machinery etc. can be replaced more quickly), a twelve-month period may only allow a few months of trading within the original Premises prior to the insurance support coming to a close. In many cases that period will not be long enough.

Of the policies with a Maximum Indemnity Period in excess of twelve-months, almost 75% have twenty-four-months cover, few insuring either beyond that or over the mid range eighteen-months.

The issue of tenancy was discussed above, and it would be prudent to assume that the rebuild time scale will be longer than for a freeholder - the tenant has no control over the rebuilding process, which will be in the hands of the landlord.

In those cases where there is a dominant customer, it is tempting to take the view that an inability to supply for even a month or two would be terminal to the business and, therefore, a Maximum Indemnity Period shorter than twelve-months might be considered appropriate.

Whereas the reference to the significant rebuild period above envisaged total destruction, that need not necessarily transpire. The majority of losses are partial losses and there is likely to be a hindrance in supplying the customer rather than a complete inability to do so. A key machine will run at 75% capacity rather than be rendered entirely defunct. The dominant customer can, therefore, potentially still be serviced, albeit at significantly higher expense in the short to medium-term. In such a situation, increased costs can be incurred to avoid Gross Profit losses arising, the policy providing critical cash flow support during the indemnity period.

Even where there is significant reliance on one or a few customers, the importance of both Gross Profit cover and an appropriately long Maximum Indemnity Period remains important.

With regards making Gross Profit declarations, if a period of eighteen-months is chosen, then the declaration should be made at 1.5 times the annual Gross Profit. A twenty-four-month period requires a declaration of double the annual figure, treble for three years and so on. The difficulties arising where the Gross Profit figure is too low have already been raised above.

For shorter Maximum Indemnity Periods, it is the case that the minimum declaration should be the annual figure. This is the case even if the Maximum Indemnity Period selected is shorter than twelve months. Paradoxically, a short Maximum Indemnity Period still requires the annual figure to be declared. Again, inadvertent under declarations can arise.

The range of issues that would suggest the need for a long Maximum Indemnity Period are wide ranging. Some of these issues have been previously raised such as the existence of listed status for buildings or the possibility of planning permission problems caused by the proximity of residential housing.

Other indicators are to some extent self-evident. The use of specialised plant and equipment with long lead times is an example, as is scarcity of replacement spares for plant which may no longer be current or may alternatively be sufficiently new that buffer stocks of spares have not yet been built-up. This has proven to be the case in the past with IT equipment where losses have occurred immediately after the purchase of the latest technology.

Seasonality of the business, scarcity of skilled staff, the importance of ambience/reputation, and reliance on any particular season's trade (as is increasingly the case with Christmas and the retail sector) are all suggestive of the need for a long Maximum Indemnity Period. This will allow at least one full season after the incident to build the business backup.

There are also businesses seeking to capitalise on one-off opportunities. A company that had gone to some lengths to produce promotional footballs for the various commercial sponsors of Euro 2000 suffered a theft of all of those samples prior to them being despatched, such that there was insufficient time to resource replacements prior to the football competition taking place. On another occasion, a business producing blank rewritable CDs, at the point that that technology first became accessible at a realistic price, suffered a fire, such that many other entrants were in the market place before their plant and equipment had been repaired. The opportunity to secure the higher selling prices that would have been available had they traded alone in the market place for an initial period were lost.

There are specific businesses where sales tend to be deferred from the point of production. IT developments which may generate royalties in later years, and whisky distilleries where a product may not be sold for twelve years, have already been noted. The answer in those cases may not be to establish a Maximum Indemnity Period running for an inordinately long time, but rather to agree a basis for measuring loss that is more meaningful and more practical.

There are situations where the results of a business will not begin to be affected as at the date of the damage, but rather at some subsequent point.

Advanced Profits cover is discussed in chapter 6, but it is noted here that such a cover allows for the commencement of the indemnity period at the date at which profit would have begun to be earned but for the Damage which has been suffered. New developments can be dealt with by the use of that extension rather than by extending the Maximum Indemnity Period unduly.

Subsidence claims do not enjoy the benefit of any explicit wording. If subsidence Damage is discovered, it may be the case that this will be monitored, perhaps through all four seasons of a year, such that repairs will not commence until after twelve months from the point at which the Damage was initially noticed. Even were there to be a keenness to effect repairs before that point, in some cases repairs could not be undertaken until it is clear how the particular building was moving.

There have been examples in the past where businesses have continued to operate normally during the monitoring period but have then had to vacate their premises or significantly curtail the extent of production during the repair period. Where this takes place more than twelve-months after the Damage is discovered, and where there is a twelve-month Maximum Indemnity Period under the business interruption insurance, then difficulties can arise.

Many insurers take the view that the twelve-month period will not start accruing until subsidence repairs actually commence, but that represents concession on the part of the insurer rather than what the policy wording actually offers. Where business interruption cover is being arranged in respect of subsidence, therefore, specific discussion should be entered into to avoid any subsequent misunderstandings.

In some cases, different subsidiary companies within a group, or even different divisions within the same company, have selected different Maximum Indemnity Periods. In some cases, where they operate totally independently, this might be appropriate. However, there have been examples where, following a claim, nobody has been able to properly explain why an affected business has a shorter period of cover than some other fellow subsidiaries.

It is not suggested that businesses should pay premium for cover that is not required, but when the reasons for the selection of a longer indemnity period for one business are considered in more detail, the underlying logic is often just as applicable to a business proposing a shorter period.

The most difficult losses to measure tend to be those for very short periods of interruption. A business suffering a power outage of a few hours or suffering Damage to one out of twenty machines may not suffer a loss significant enough to produce a noticeable variance in the monthly management accounts. Very short actual indemnity periods take an inordinate amount of management time to investigate and quantify and it is suggested that consideration be given to exclude such losses either via a time or monetary excess under a policy, or alternatively by using a franchise. The franchise operates in precisely the same as an excess, except that if the figure selected is exceeded, then the whole amount becomes payable without any monetary or time deduction. To make such an approach worthwhile, of course, there has to be a premium benefit available which the insurer involved may or may not find difficult to justify when all of the other factors affecting the business are also taken into consideration.

Engineering breakdown cover is discussed below, but the relevance of raising it here is that Maximum Indemnity Periods for engineering policies tend to be significantly shorter than those under general commercial policies. The logic of such an approach has perhaps historically been based upon the assumption that plant and machinery will be built robustly, with a view to ongoing repairs and maintenance allowing it to remain functional for many years. In theory, breakdowns could, therefore, be repaired relatively easily in contrast to, say, general fire, or flood Damage, against which most businesses choose a twelve-month Maximum Indemnity Period. It is particularly important to review the logic of selecting a short Maximum Indemnity Period when the cover relates to a critical machine through which a significant proportion of production passes. If a twelve-month cover is deemed to be appropriate should fire Damage be suffered, it might prove to be imprudent to have only three months cover for a breakdown event which in some circumstances could still cause a significant reduction in turnover.

In recommending the adoption of longer Maximum Indemnity Periods generally, there comes a point after an insured event where other, unrelated, influences gradually achieve more prominence than the Damage itself. It might be the case, for example, after say three years that there will be a difficulty in continuing to identify losses flowing solely from the insured event. As a generality, therefore, many businesses would not be encouraged to adopt a Maximum Indemnity Period exceeding three years. Potential exceptions even to this observation might be luxury hotels or fashionable bars or bistros who may take a very significant period of time to build business backup to the previous level. That could be the case where the patrons are wealthy and place a premium on service and quality in preference to price.

6. Expanding the Core Cover

Overview

The core business interruption cover relates to Damage from an insured peril to property used for the purpose of the business at the Premises.

In many cases, it might be desirable to arrange for cover from insured events at other locations, such as those of customers or suppliers. In a sense, these extensions expand the concept of Premises.

In other instances, additional perils can be insured against at the Premises already identified, expanding the scope of the existing cover. Engineering breakdown is an example.

Further, there are extensions that do not fit either of the above categories, not being related to fixed locations, nor introducing new perils at the Premises themselves. Denial of Access and Loss of Attraction cover are examples of this, dealing with events that might occur in the locality of the Premises, albeit still requiring Damage in the vicinity.

The most commonly required extensions have been considered below.

Additional Increase in Cost of Working

The core business interruption cover provides for increased costs to be incurred to avoid a loss of Gross Profit, but not exceeding the amount of the profit loss thereby avoided (the economic limit). It is possible to extend the insurance such that any amount of money can be spent as long as it is reasonable and necessary for the business, without reference to any such economic limit, and this is what the Additional Increase in Cost of Working cover offers. The standard wording is as follows:

"The insurance ... is limited to:
The additional expenditure necessarily and reasonably incurred by the insured as a consequence of the incident in order to prevent or minimise the interruption of or interference of the business during the Indemnity Period."

There are no underinsurance provisions applying to this cover – it represents a maximum claimable amount (a limit of indemnity).

Specialist suppliers, or those dealing with luxury goods, might value their reputation sufficiently that they would wish to spend more money than a particular transaction is worth to ensure that the service to the customer does not suffer. In the case of a retailer, the value of the transaction from a particular member of the public may offer a low economic limit without this policy extension.

Businesses at the opposite end of the spectrum can also benefit from the cover. Where margins are very low, as is the case with petrol forecourt sales, for milkmen and for many other commoditised businesses, very low economic limits might preclude the accrual of significant increased costs under the core policy wording. Such businesses rely on a volume of transactions rather than high profitability from each one.

There are other businesses, such as franchises, or those having to satisfy quality control standards or British Standards to be on a customer supply panel, who may have to incur significant costs other than expenditure related directly to production. Formula One racing teams are required to participate in minimum numbers of races each year, and in some cases it can be difficult to establish whether there would be revenue or profit reductions were the expenditure not to be incurred.

It should be noted that the Additional Increase in Cost of Working cover is still subject to other facets of normal increased cost cover. Where an asset is purchased, for example, to help mitigate a loss (such as an extra distribution vehicle, or forklift truck) or where a lease has been taken out where the lessor requires a minimum lease period significantly exceeding the Maximum Indemnity Period under the policy, then residual values will still have to be calculated. In the case of an additional delivery vehicle, this could be sold at the end of the Maximum Indemnity Period. The amount claimable from the insurer would then be the difference between the purchase price and sales proceeds (net of costs).

Additionally, there must still be a benefit produced within the Maximum Indemnity Period - significant expenditure on advertising on the last day of the Maximum Indemnity Period would be no more admissible than is the case with a standard Increase in Cost of Working cover.

Finally, it is the case that costs must still be incurred to mitigate interruption resulting from Damage. The limitations in accepting penalties required under a contract as standard Increased Costs of Working would also be relevant to an Additional Increase in Cost of Working cover. As a rule of thumb, if the insured business has no choice but to incur a cost it is unlikely to be covered under either a Standard Increase in Cost of Working or Additional Increased Cost of Working cover.

There are businesses that take the view that Gross Profit cover is not required and arrange business interruption policies with Increase in Cost of Working cover only. This has been the case in the past with high street retailers, manufacturers and others.

Invariably, the claims experience suggests that Gross Profit losses cannot be totally avoided, notwithstanding that the judicious expenditure of increased costs can mitigate the same. The presumption that a Board of Directors is sufficiently gifted that any problem can be resolved without any Gross Profit loss arising if only sufficient funds are available to spend has been demonstrated, in the majority of cases, to be wrong. In some cases, businesses cannot incur an increased cost at all.

For example, it might not be possible to subcontract work. Increasingly, the claims experience confirms that the reducing number of businesses operating in various parts of the manufacturing sector is producing difficulty in sourcing subcontractors who are both willing and have the capacity to take on work in the short to medium-term. For a partial loss affecting a business already running twenty-four hours per day, seven days per week, or where staff are unwilling or unable to work overtime then a desire on the part of directors to incur expenditure to protect their position may be frustrated.

The Supply Chain

It has been previously observed that incidents occurring at the premises of a supplier or customer can produce just as significant an impact on the insured business as an incident occuring at the Premises.

A customer's or supplier's extension provides that loss "resulting from interruption of or interference with the Business in consequence of loss, destruction or damage at the under noted situations or to properties undernoted shall be deemed to be an Incident" as if it occurred at the Premises.

The cover will relate either to specific customers/suppliers, or it will be a general cover relating to all customers/suppliers, subject to limits of loss. For specified suppliers/customers the relevant premises (in the United Kingdom or Northern Ireland) will be specifically listed.

In the case of the general covers, these relate to "suppliers, manufacturers or processors of components, goods or materials" (for suppliers extensions) and for customers with whom there is an existing relationship (i.e. not prospective customers) in United Kingdom or Northern Ireland.

There will also be inner limits applicable to the unspecified covers as for the specified customer or supplier extensions. In the case of the latter, specific limits will be selected by the insured business and the premium charged accordingly. In the case of unspecified customers in practice a 10% limit of the sum insured in any one period would typically apply.

It is worth appreciating that territorial limits applicable to these extensions comprise United Kingdom/Northern Ireland and these extensions will, therefore, not assist with regards overseas customers in the absence of any specific further discussion.

Additionally, it is common in practice to find that only a restricted range of insured perils will be provided in relation to the customers'/suppliers' premises. Not all incidents that might be covered at the Premises themselves (under an All Risks cover, for example) would be dealt with if they occurred at the third party sites.

There is a requirement for an insured event (loss, destruction or damage) to occur at the suppliers/customers premises giving rise to interruption or interference with the business. General, non-specific interruptions are not covered. Some evidence of the nature of the incident suffered by the customer/supplier will be needed in practice.

Notwithstanding the preceding observation, there is no specific requirement for the customer or supplier themselves to have adequate insurance covering the incident or indeed any insurance at all. The insurance arrangements of the customer or supplier are not relevant.

In terms of the operation of the policy, a suppliers extension specifically excludes public utilities covers in the standard Association of British Insurers wording and in many wordings in practice - such extensions are available separately. Some newer services may not be explicitly excluded. Internet service providers, for example, may fall within the definition of suppliers. Whether they do or not, the significance of a website not being available due to an incident at the Internet service provider's premises is one which is just as likely to impact upon the insured business as an incident at the premises of a supplier.

The need for a customers or suppliers extension is generally self apparent. An over reliance on any one customer or supplier suggests the need for this cover. Only the insured business is in a position to know that such trading relationships exist. If these are not disclosed to the broker and/or insurer, then avoidable shortfalls in the scope of policy cover may arise.

In practice, there are many situations where claims are not made under unspecified suppliers or customers covers which at face value would be dealt with by the relevant policies if submitted. This would seem to derive from a general lack of awareness of what the policy cover offers and there have been cases where significant incidents have caused the insolvency of suppliers due to the fact that no orders for raw materials are placed with the supplier until the fire damage is repaired. The supplier may be unable to survive an uninsured but significant loss of turnover. On at least one occasion it has become apparent retrospectively that suppliers in these situations have had unspecified customers extensions but were unaware of the fact. This can be easily be done if cover was not specifically requested at inception, but was nevertheless included as part of a commercial combined insurer.

There is a premium cost in purchasing such customers and/or suppliers extensions. To make sure that the solvency of suppliers, at least, will not be compromised following an insured incident, it might be prudent to request confirmation, in advance of any incident, that they have arranged an appropriate customer's extension under their insurance cover. The cost of arranging that will be borne by them, albeit it will ultimately be transferred back via the pricing structure.

Advanced Profits

The standard business interruption policy provides cover over a defined period (the Maximum Indemnity Period) commencing from the date of the Damage. This is appropriate for existing income streams, but is clearly not so for an income stream which will commence in the future.

A landlord may be arranging for the construction of new premises to rent out, or a manufacturing business may be building a new factory. In either case, Damage to assets will not impact upon the profit and loss account of the business until the point at which revenue/profit would have started to be generated but for the incident.

This is acknowledged by a revised definition of the indemnity period under an Advanced Profits Cover (as opposed to that in the standard policy wording):

"The period beginning with the date upon which, but for the Damage, Turnover would have commenced to be earned and ending not later than the Maximum Indemnity Period thereafter during which the results of the business shall be affected in consequence of the Damage."

It follows that there should be an ascertainable date upon which the profit stream would have occurred but for the Damage. This should in theory be easy to establish with reference to construction project plans, delivery schedules for plant and equipment etc.

There is another reason for arranging an Advanced Profits Cover in addition to the deferred commencement of loss. The standard cover will operate when there has been Damage to assets owned or used by the insured business for the purpose of that business at the Premises. Where there are assets in the course of construction, these may not have been handed over to the insured business by contractors at the time that they suffer Damage. The business will, therefore, neither own nor use them. Under a standard wording the Material Damage Proviso will not be satisfied by Damage to assets neither owned nor used for the purpose of the business, and the business interruption cover would not ordinarily be available.

It is not always clear when an Advanced Profits cover is required. Where there is the addition of one extra machine to a line of thirteen existing machines, and where the lead time of purchase is not significant then the standard business interruption cover (assuming an appropriate Maximum Indemnity Period has been selected) is likely to be sufficient.

At the other extreme, the construction of a new factory on a new site will certainly require an Advanced Profits Cover. Between these two poles the situation can be less clear.

Where a business is extending its manufacturing capacity at existing premises, the financial budgets for the coming year will reflect the investment in such assets within the forecast turnover figures. These investments, and the additional capacity that they represent would be considered when calculating Standard Turnover for settlement purposes, albeit the period under consideration would still commence from the date of Damage rather than from the date on which the income stream from the extended capacity would otherwise have commenced.

There is a practical issue to be considered when arranging Advanced Profits Cover and that is the assessment of the insurable amount. Any significant capital expenditure would usually be accompanied by the preparation of a business plan justifying such expenditure in terms of the turnover and profit that will subsequently be generated by it. There can be dissatisfaction on the part of an insured business if the forecast was accepted at face value for premium purposes but is subsequently considered to be an unsatisfactory and unreliable basis to establish quantum if a claim is made.

This contrasts with the majority of claims, where the declaration made at the start of a policy period can be compared to actual (historical) financial performance (which will often be supported by VAT returns or third party documentation). With a development that has not yet started there may be little to support quantum other than the initial forecast. Prior to arranging Advanced Profits cover, therefore, and to avoid an expectation difficulty, it is advisable for the insured business to discuss in detail with the insurer/broker the basis of settlement should an insured event occur.

That is not to suggest that forecasts are of no value. For those businesses with a reasonable financial history, it will be possible to validate the accuracy of forecasting and budgeting generally. A parallel situation in terms of assessment of profitability of a new department can be found with regards new businesses. The New Business clause acknowledges that a historical financial record may not exist for new businesses suffering insured incidents and in effect accepts that the best estimate, based on what is available, will have to be used in agreeing settlement of any claim.

The mechanics of the operation of the Advanced Profits cover parallel the standard wording. Standard Turnover reflects the turnover which would have been generated but for the Damage within the Maximum Indemnity Period. As previously noted, that period begins when production would have commenced but for the Damage. The Rate of Gross Profit is the rate that would have been generated within that future period.

There is a slight anomaly when it comes to increased costs. The indemnity period for an Advanced Profits Cover will not commence until the date on which the profit would have begun to have been generated but for the Damage.

If a fire affects assets under construction, there may be a desire to incur premium costs to accelerate repairs so that the commencement of production is as close to the original plan as possible. If these costs are incurred, that would, therefore, be before the commencement of the Maximum Indemnity Period.

Technically, increased costs incurred prior to commencement of the indemnity period would not fall for consideration. The wording provides no cover for such costs in accelerating repairs to bring the date on which profit begins to be generated back toward the date initially anticipated. Equally paradoxically, any savings in costs prior to the initially anticipated commencement date (but for the insured event) would not accrue to insurer's benefit.

In reality, it will be preferable to avoid significant gross profit losses if increased expenditure can be incurred to mitigate them. However, after discussion, even if there is a concession on the part of insurers to deal with increased costs incurred prior to commencement of the indemnity period, there will still be a delay whilst the forecast figures are investigated. This will inevitably take longer than assessing Standard Turnover under a claim at the Premises due to the absence of historical trade figures relating to the new element of business.

The need for the insured business to communicate, as rapidly as possible, any proposed mitigation plan to allow the merits to be considered is, therefore, significant. It can be a good idea to discuss with the insured business (at the time that an Advanced Profits Cover is being arranged) whether any additional costs could be expended if an incident were to occur, and if so, what sort of cost is envisaged. Discussion can then take place with the insurers to avoid misunderstandings at claims time and to establish that there is consistency in intent as to what the cover is addressing between the insured business and the insurer.

Utilities Extensions

The Utilities Extensions available expand the cover to deal with incidents away from the Premises and also in effect extend the range of perils.

There are two distinct extensions available to insure utilities.

The first extension covers loss (as insured by the policy) resulting from loss, destruction or Damage at the land based Premises of utility suppliers, be that an electricity, gas, water or telecommunications business. The cover will be restricted to United Kingdom or Northern Ireland and it is common in practice, if not in the standard wordings, for a restricted range of perils to be insured against.

This extension requires an incident to occur at the premises of utility providers and will require Damage to occur there which causes the failure in supply.

In practical terms, it is very unusual for claims to be paid under this particular extension. This is partly because supply can be re-routed by the utility company, to some extent, following any failure at land based premises. More importantly, the majority of power failure claims occur because of an incident in between the generating station and the insured's Premises, affecting the cabling, for example, as far as electricity is concerned.

It is relevant to note that the term 'Premises' has been held to include inspection pits set in the pavements to allow access to gas/electric installations and that cover is, therefore, wider than if it related just to those demised Premises on which buildings stand.

The second type of utility extension covers interruption or interference with the business due to accidental failure of the utility (electricity/gas/water/telecommunications) at the point of supply at the premises of the insured business. This will be the main stop cock in the case of water, the supply authority's meter in the case of gas and the terminal ends for the case of electricity.

Accidental damage to cabling particularly near railways or canals is common (due, in the case of canals to the concentration of services at bridging points).

The overwhelming majority of utility claims are dealt with under this latter extension. If an insured business identifies the need for cover in relation to failure of a utility, this will most effectively be achieved through this extension rather than the alternative covering the premises of the supply authority only.

It is worth noting that there are defined points in the supply cabling/pipework, prior to which the incident must occur for cover under this extension to be available. The logic of this is that if there is damage beyond those points they would comprise property for which the insured is responsible and would generate a standard material damage claim which would in turn satisfy the Material Damage Proviso and allow a 'normal' business interruption claim to be made. There are cases where care should be taken in assuming that the applicability will be black and white. Shopping malls, for example, may involve a failure in utility supply to tenants' shops even though there has not been a failure in supply to the mall overall. Were it to have been previously argued, after a fire within the mall, for example, that the Premises should be deemed to be the mall in its entirety, rather than merely the tenant's shop, then such an argument can cause difficulty when the utility claim is presented. Clearly, there has to be consistency in defining whether the Premises should be deemed to refer to the whole mall or just the tenant's shop for the purpose of triggering business interruption cover, regardless of the type of incident arising.

There may be a time excess or franchise. Short Maximum Indemnity Periods will commonly be arranged compared to the main perils of fire, flood etc. Such shorter periods acknowledge that interruptions in utility supply will usually be of very limited duration. Business interruption losses will generally be more limited than those arising from fires or floods.

However, scenarios could arise threatening call centres, for example, with medium to long-term loss if there is a telecommunication failure at a critical point in the sales cycle. Individually significant customers could withdraw their business indefinitely. Confirmation that the Maximum Indemnity Period is acceptably long at inception can avoid subsequent misunderstanding.

The telecommunications cover should be considered not merely in terms of telephony but more importantly in terms of data transfer, Internet use and digital communication generally. The risks that digital aspects of commerce present is discussed below to allow more detailed consideration of the matter.

In passing, it is worthwhile noting that there are significant exclusions particular to the utilities extensions, most notably any deliberate act of the supply authority. Failure at the terminal ends will not be covered if the electricity company, for example, isolated supply to allow necessary work to take place.

Finally, it should be noted that the utilities extensions extend the business interruption rather than the material damage cover. Spoilage of stock and work in progress following a power failure would not be claimable under this extension, albeit it could be addressed separately as part of the material damage section of the policy. This is consistent with stock spoilage arising after fire or flood, for example.

Denial of Access

The Association of British Insurers standard wording is as follows:

"Property in the vicinity of the Premises, loss or destruction of or damage to which shall prevent or hinder the use of the Premises or access thereto, whether the Premises or property of the insured therein shall be damaged or not, but excluding loss or destruction of or damage to property of any

supply undertaking from which the insured obtains electricity, gas, water or telecommunication services which prevents or hinders the supply of such services, to the premises."

There is a requirement for a specific event to have occurred and for damage to have affected property in the vicinity. There is no cover for contractors carrying out maintenance work on roads or utilities in the vicinity, or access restrictions having been granted by the local authority to allow for adjacent construction work, for example.

Some package policies available provide Denial of Access Cover as a matter of course, extending the cover from the standard cover, which requires damage at the premises, to business interruption claims following damage at or near the premises.

The term vicinity is undefined, but a potential radius from the premises of as much as twenty-five miles can be inferred from case law. The issue is the extent to which a direct link can be established between the location of damage and the Premises rather than a strict distance between the two.

Consider a café serving tourists on an island linked to the mainland by one bridge five miles away from the café. Damage to the linking bridge would probably be considered to have occurred within the vicinity. On the other hand, damage to a location five miles from premises readily accessible from a number of directions and arterial routes might not be considered to be in the vicinity. The merits of any particular case would have to be considered.

Importantly, whilst this extension is often referred to as the denial or prevention of access, the cover is more extensive than that, allowing for hindrance of the use of the premises or access thereto.

A hindrance is not qualified or quantified nor is there differentiation between vehicle or pedestrian use. A hindrance resulting from damage in the vicinity will, therefore, trigger the cover just as much as a total denial. (It would still be necessary to be able to demonstrate that any depression in trading figures could be related to the hindrance. In the same way that satisfaction of the Material Damage Proviso will not allow a claim for loss not flowing from Damage to succeed, there must still be a causative affect. The identification of some form of hindrance will not in itself allow a claim for all and any variation in the business subsequent to that event.)

Sometimes, it can be difficult to conclude that a hindrance has occurred or continues to occur. Consider the following situation:

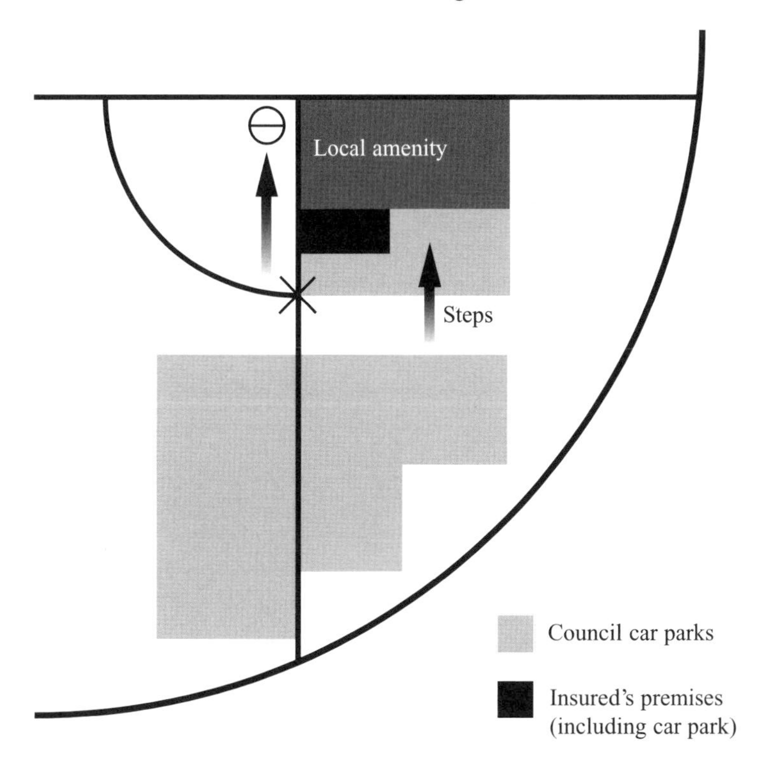

The above diagram represents part of a city centre. The radial circular route is an inner ring road. Shoppers would commonly use the car parks immediately within the inner ring road to walk to the central shopping malls circa five minutes away. The local amenity is a theatre offering matinee and evening performances. Its opening hours are mirrored by the insured business offering coffee and light snacks throughout the day and Tex-Mex dining in the evening.

Damage occurred at the point marked 'X', the entrance to a one way street that ran past the insured restaurant and up past the theatre. As a consequence of the damage, the street could not be accessed. After around four hours pedestrians were allowed to walk up the street, scaffolding having been erected with wood planking over the top to prevent any debris falling upon the public. Vehicle access was not possible. After around two weeks the no entry sign at the other end of the road was suspended. (Council employees taped a black bin liner over the sign.) Temporary signs were placed at either end of the street confirming the new and temporary arrangement, but these were frequently moved by youths. After one month the scaffolding was eventually removed and both vehicles and pedestrians were allowed access.

Pedestrians, it should be noted, could have accessed the car park immediately adjacent to the insured business by using some steps which were around fifteen metres away from the point of damage.

Clearly, there was never a total denial of access to the premises of the insured Business. Pedestrians at least were able to walk the wrong way down the one way street and access it at all times without restriction. As far as hindrance is concerned, it could be argued that pedestrians could have used the alternative steps and walked across the car park without any difficulty to the insured business. That, however, presupposed that they knew about the nearby steps (their existence was not obvious due to the positioning of a wall). It was accepted that the blockage at one end of the road to pedestrians did constitute a hindrance. It was further accepted that both the initial and subsequent hindrance of cars reaching the premises via the altered road priorities meant that the cover should deal with the losses throughout the period. The ongoing denial of access to vehicles, notwithstanding that pedestrians could very quickly after the incident access the area in the normal manner, was sufficient.

Whilst not directly pertinent to the case set out above, a scenario could be envisaged where Damage to the adjacent theatre could still give rise to a Denial of Access claim on the part of the restaurant. This could, however, be exacerbated by loss flowing due to the absence of the theatre. This latter element of loss, to the extent that it could be quantified, could not be dealt with without a Loss of Attraction extension.

On another occasion, an insured business constituted a clubhouse (bar/restaurant) within a static caravan site. A raised roadway ran from the site entrance to the clubhouse. Following torrential rain and flooding, the site became extremely muddy and waterlogged, such that vehicles could drive along the road to the clubhouse but could not realistically leave the road to reach the static caravans without becoming severely bogged down. Pedestrians with suitable wellington boots could have accessed the static caravans.

Unfortunately, in this particular case, there was no hindrance of access to the insured business itself. It could be reached via the raised roadway. It was suggested that the whole of the site should be considered the Premises. This did not assist, as access to the site from the main road could be easily achieved. In terms of the whole site, there was a denial of access within, rather than to it. In that particular case the insurance cover was unable to assist.

The issue of defining the Premises was raised in terms of the utility extension above and care should be taken to be consistent in the definition of Premises. Whether the case at hand concerns a clubhouse on the static caravan park or a retail unit within a shopping mall, clarity between insured business and insurer as to what will be deemed to be the Premises for the purpose of considering the application of business interruption cover (consistently, regardless of peril) is advisable.

It should be noted that this cover relates to a physical hindrance or denial of access. A disinclination to visit the premises is not sufficient.

Loss of Attraction

A standard wording will deal with interruption to and interference with the business in relation to *'Property in the vicinity of the Premises, destruction of or damage to which will cause loss of custom to the insured directly due to loss of amenities in the immediate vicinity of the Premises whether the Premises or property of the insured therein shall be damaged or not'*.

This cover will be highly relevant where a business relies on the presence of neighbouring facilities to generate its income. Restaurants located next to theatres can rely on the latter for much of their income. Shops can enjoy passing trade because of the presence of a major retail chain. Cafés may be supported by the business of employees of a major local manufacturer - there are many examples that could be cited. In these cases, the absence of the source of attraction could produce losses as significant as Damage at the Premises themselves and the need for this extension should be seriously considered.

As with the denial/prevention of access cover, 'vicinity' is not defined, although the word 'immediate' is placed before it in this wording. Whilst that still does not quantify the term, it suggests an intention to restrict the scope of cover compared to the Denial of Access extension.

In arranging a loss of attraction cover the insured business would almost certainly have identified the attraction that it is seeking cover against and, to avoid any misunderstanding, this can be specifically identified to insurers with its proximity clearly stated to avoid any difficulty at claims time.

Loss of attraction cover relates to the loss of a neighbouring attraction rather than a depression in the attractiveness of the business itself. Following an insured event, a business may suffer from competitors' gossip and a loss of reputation or a blemishing thereof may result. Gossip/blemishing are not insured events. Loss arising from gossip would not be covered albeit it is not specifically excluded either. Where the gossip arises coterminously with Damage that is otherwise insured, if the separate financial impact of the gossiping cannot be identified then the whole loss will be dealt with.

In very rare cases, it can be demonstrated that any impact on the business arises solely from gossip. Consider the following example:

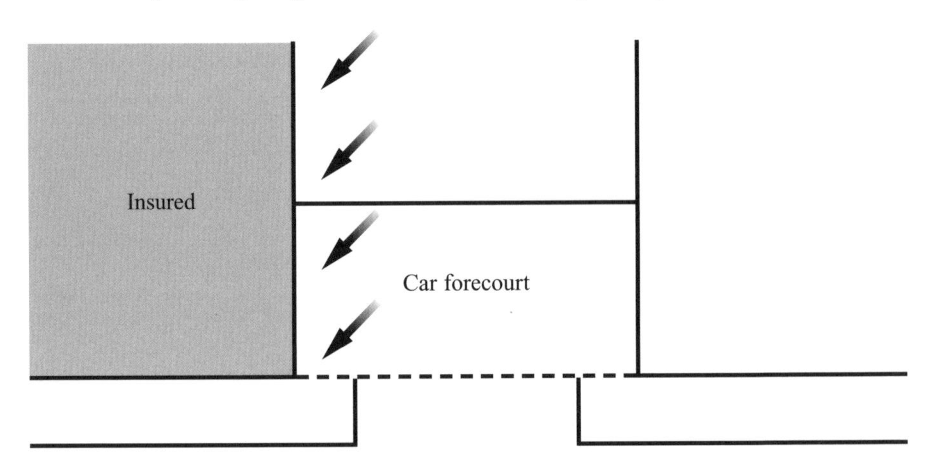

Fire damage to insured premises from neighbour

In this case, there was a fire in a car showroom and to vehicles on a car forecourt which was adjacent to the insured business which sold three-piece suites and other furniture to the public on the high street of an urban satellite. The fire damage to the car showroom caused damage to the side of the building that the insured business occupied and which they owned, albeit no smoke penetrated inside. From the front of the Premises it would not be apparent that the furniture business had suffered any loss at all. Local radio nevertheless reported that there had been very severe damage to the furniture retailer and there was a significant drop in turnover and gross profit as a consequence.

The material damage proviso had been satisfied (there had been external Damage to the side of the building). However, no smoke or other damage was visible either from the front or the inside of the Premises and the loss could, therefore, only be attributed to the gossip and the local press reports. No payment was made by insurers.

Such an instance is very rare. The reduction in turnover flowing from Damage, and that exacerbated by gossip cannot usually be distinguished. The example is nevertheless offered for completeness. Damage to reputation is not something that can currently be covered. Damage to a business' brand is currently addressed through the selection of an appropriately long Maximum Indemnity Period (if the brand is damaged, that will manifest itself in reduced turnover).

Engineering Policies

An engineering policy offers three heads of cover, being: Breakdown, Accidental Damage and Loss of Utilities.

1. Breakdown

The desire for breakdown cover is invariably the main reason for the engineering policy being incepted. Breakdown would not be covered under a standard policy wording - it would simply not constitute an insured event of loss or Damage.

Breakdown cover is not a replacement for a proper maintenance program. Gradually operating causes and wear and tear issues will be excluded. There is an ongoing need to arrange necessary statutory inspections of plant and to observe any maintenance regime represented to insurers at inception. It should be noted that there is a need to not only carry out the maintenance but to evidence the same. A failure to do so can produce a difficulty if the nature of a breakdown is uncertain. The evidence of a planned maintenance regime can bring clarity and assist prompt resolution of a claim.

2. Accidental Damage
The type of incident which will give rise to a claim under the Accidental Damage cover would already be dealt with by an All Risks policy. The need for accidental damage is therefore likely only to be necessary if the commercial combined policy has been written on a Perils rather than on an All Risks basis.

The cover relates to sudden and unforeseen Damage arising from an accidental cause. Gradually arising causes and wear and tear are again excluded. It should also be noted that the cover relates to plant at the Premises. A separate transit cover would need to be arranged if the plant was being moved. In the past, significant Damage has been caused to plant taken off site for maintenance. Such damage, not occurring at the Premises, is not covered.

3. Utilities
Utility extensions are available as part of the general commercial cover, as has been previously discussed. The availability of utility cover under an engineering policy allows the extension to be related to a specific machine rather than the Premises generally, which may sometimes provide a premium advantage.

Relating the cover to specific machines will also be the case with regards breakdown and accidental damage. These relate to specific pieces of plant rather than being a general floating cover over the whole of the plant and equipment of the Premises.

There are two specific aspects of Engineering policies that are not found under standard commercial combined covers.

Firstly, Maximum Indemnity Periods are often very much shorter than for the core policy. Three months would be typical, with a range of between one and six months commonly taken out. The logic of a three month Maximum Indemnity Period for breakdown compared to a much longer period for Damage caused by fire, for example, acknowledges the potentially wider scope of damage that the latter might represent.

There is also an assumption, however, that Damage to a specific machine can be repaired more easily and quickly than general fire or flood damage. This was certainly the case historically, when manufacturing businesses employed maintenance staff who would be able to provide labour and the expertise to effect repairs. The need to obtain spare parts was the only cause of delay.

It is now the case in many industries, given that plant and equipment has become increasingly sophisticated, that scope for internal maintenance can be limited and suppliers need to be relied upon. There may be a limited availability of spare parts, and also a need to wait for a machine supplier's specialist labour to install the same when they are available.

The impact of these factors (which parallels the increase in sophistication of motor cars limiting the ability of the domestic enthusiast to carry out his own maintenance) is that the need for an appropriately long Maximum Indemnity Period under an Engineering policy is just as important as for a general commercial combined policy. Three month periods are increasingly proving to be insufficient.

Secondly, the engineering policy cover typically incorporates an excess period in terms of time rather than a finite monetary amount. (This may be a franchise rather than an excess whereby the whole of the loss is payable if the stated time is exceeded without any deduction, whereas an excess will be deducted regardless of the duration of the incident.) It is not usually explicitly stated whether the period of excess/franchise commences with the occurrence of the Damage or with the occurrence of the business interruption loss.

Consider an incident occurring at 5.00pm on a Friday night for a business which does not commonly work weekends. If there is a forty-eight hour excess period, in chronological terms, that period expired over the Saturday/Sunday when no production would have taken place regardless of the incident. It is the case generally that the policy wording should be taken at face value and using everyday interpretation of the language, unless there is ambiguity or a specific need to do otherwise. A forty-eight hour excess, therefore, should run chronologically from the point of the damage in the same way as a Maximum Indemnity Period commences from the point of the Damage.

There might be a temptation, following an incident, for increased costs to be deferred until after an excess period has expired. This does not avoid the application of the excess. If gross profit losses immediately after an incident are not payable because of a time excess, any increased costs incurred (at any time) to avoid such losses would by definition be uneconomic. It is the timing of the gross profit loss that is important, not the timing of the increased costs. As a corollary, increased costs incurred within an excess period to mitigate gross profit losses thereafter would be payable.

It is of note that aspects of risk that may be particularly relevant to the general commercial insurer may be viewed as a virtue rather than a vice by the engineering insurer. Consider a business manufacturing pine furniture. The availability of significant quantities of buffer stock may comprise a risk from the fire insurer's point of view. The engineering insurer will welcome the presence of buffer stock regardless of the raw material involved, as it represents an opportunity to mitigate any Gross Profit loss presenting itself. On the other hand, the presence of sprinklers might bring a more favourable view from a fire insurer but may be irrelevant to the engineering breakdown insurer.

It should be noted that this cover is a business interruption cover and following a breakdown, as with a cessation of electric supply under a utilities extension, any spoilage of stock in process will not give rise to a payment relating to the stock itself. Solidification of plastic pellets within an extrusion line could be a problem, as could solidification of metal in casting pots or moulds. Such material damage wastage is not covered.

Finally, there is the issue of concurrent causes of loss. If a machine head crashes due to wear and tear failure of a ball bearing there may be subsequent impact damage on the machine bed. Subsequent impact damage would be insured but the wear and tear failure would be excluded. In the majority of situations the insured cause runs beyond and overrides the excluded cause such that the whole loss will be payable. There are occasions, however, where replacement of the part suffering the wear and tear failure has taken longer than the repair of the insured damage. In such a situation the exclusion would override entirely giving rise to no payment being due from insurers.

Fines & Penalties

A payment which has to be made to a customer because of an historic contract would not, as has been previously observed, fall for consideration as an Increased Cost of Working. It would be incurred primarily because of an historic contract and not solely to avoid a future reduction in turnover. Neither would it be covered as an Additional Increase in Cost of Working. It would not be reasonably and necessarily incurred to avoid future interruption to the business but, again, because of the existence of the historic contract.

If it is the intention to insure against contractual penalties then a fines and penalties extension will have to be added to the policy. This item will be subject to a separate Limit of Indemnity relating to payments which are legally liable to be paid for any breach of contract in consequence of an incident.

One group of businesses which most obviously have an exposure to contractual penalties are those firms delivering to automotive manufacturers' tracksides, where hourly fines of up to £30,000 might be applicable if a supply failure halts production. If it were intended to protect against the consequences of an incident over a twelve-month Maximum Indemnity Period, the amount at risk per hour on a 24/7 basis would amount to some £262 million. The premium on that amount might exceed the annual profit generated by the business and might not be a tenable undertaking.

The cost of insuring contractual penalties of this magnitude as part of the insurance programme is not economic and would be better addressed as part of the firm's wider risk management.

That is not to say that a lower level of indemnity covering a shorter period is not advisable, but in the car manufacturing example, that would still amount to some £60,000,000 for a three month period, the shorter Maximum Indemnity Period commonly envisaged under an engineering policy. Even £1,000,000 of cover would only represent just over a day's production.

Many businesses do not face contractual penalties of this magnitude, and for them addressing the risk as part of the insurance programme might be tenable. The level of indemnity will, by definition, be dictated by the largest contractual exposure with a customer. The insured business should be able to establish this without difficulty and premium quotations can be obtained. The economics of insuring or dealing with the risk any other way can then be considered.

In the absence of formal written contracts, it may still be the case that the custom and practice of a particular industry does entail payments to customers where disruption is caused to them, whether by an event insured or not. In that situation, the penalty payments would be a contractual matter albeit not one evidenced in writing. This may be the case with supermarkets who may demand payments representing the profit that they would have been achieved on the sale of product on the shelves (notwithstanding that other products would have filled the shelf space and generated alternative profit). Whilst such claims could be resisted both on liability and quantum grounds, contractual payments may still have to be made if that is the custom.

Research & Development

Research often represents the investigation or application of new technologies, or qualities of materials, or general experimentation, with broad objectives which, if met, would allow further investigatory work to be undertaken.

That is to be contrasted with development work which is generally intended to apply the generic research and develop specific new products for sale.

In the pharmaceutical industry, development work may follow reasonably quickly after research, or may offer itself as an unforeseen side effect as part of research focused in another direction. The development of Viagra tablets is an example of this, that product being developed on the back of research that was initially intended to deal with heart conditions.

Where the development period is relatively short, and where the Maximum Indemnity Period is appropriately long, Damage which affects the project at the Premises may be largely covered under the existing Gross Profit cover - development costs are unlikely to be have been uninsured.

If development work is subcontracted to third party premises, in whole or in part, then an incident could occur there which would not trigger policy cover as the Material Damage Proviso might not be satisfied. From the point of view of the insured business that would most ideally be covered by extending the definition of premises albeit at the expense of a reduced range of perils and subject to an inner limit.

Research has a less direct focus and, in common with longer product development periods, ongoing research may not give rise to turnover generation potentially for years. Damage affecting the research assets is, therefore, unlikely to produce a reduction in turnover or any payment under the Gross Profit item. If no Gross Profit is at risk, then by definition no increased costs could be paid as they would automatically be uneconomic.

To address this, a separate item with a limit of indemnity could be arranged in respect of research and development which would typically pay a pro rata proportion of the annual research and expenditure cost on a weekly basis, subject to a Maximum Indemnity Period. The cover would allow for the recreation of research that has been lost and which has to be recreated.

In those situations where the research represents the creation of data which itself is properly backed up and saved off site then the need for recreation may be reduced. Ongoing laboratory testing could be lost as could hard copy statistical surveys or analysis. The ease of replacement of both information gained from research and of the assets used in the research department generally will dictate the need for this extension.

Difficulty has been experienced in the past in replacing sophisticated laser and other electronic systems for which there can be lead times of many months. In the case of universities, damage to research equipment may require the recreation of work already undertaken (particularly if a repeat of any earlier trials is necessary to comply with proper validation or quality control). However, there is also an income issue if grants are received to support the education of students in the relevant department, or where commercial sponsorship might be jeopardised if the research is interrupted.

It is recommended that the time scale for replacement of significant pieces of plant in a research department is considered in precisely the same way as for production departments. The ease of replacement of data developed should also be discussed and the existence of any income streams which might be jeopardised properly identified.

The latter would not be addressed through a standard research and development wording, which offers support for costs incurred but not for any ongoing loss of income. It could be appropriate to include any such grants or sponsorship monies within the definition of turnover, slightly altering the standard wording to ensure that there is no shortfall at claims time.

Outbreak of Notifiable Disease

This extension provides cover for any *'loss resulting from interruption of or interference with the Business carried on by the insured at the Premises'* in respect of:

1) An outbreak of a notifiable disease at the Premises/within twenty-five miles of the Premises, or of the discovery of an organism likely to give rise to such a disease.

2) The discovery of vermin/pests at the Premises causing a restriction on the order or advice of a local authority.

3) An accident or defect in the drains causing restrictions on the order of a local authority.

4) The occurrence of murder/suicide at the Premises. Hotels, cafés and restaurants clearly need such cover as do schools, hospitals and leisure centres/swimming pools. On a much wider basis, any business involved with the production or distribution of food should give careful consideration to the need to extend the basic policy wording in this way.

There are defined lists of diseases in respect of which local authorities are able to act and it should be noted that only the diseases falling into those categories would trigger policy cover. There have been cases in the past where local authorities have extended their remit and restricted the activities of a business in respect of a non notifiable disease. A compliant business may then seek reimbursement of losses from insurers, only to find that cover is unavailable. A clear understanding of the scope and limitations of the cover at inception is essential. Non notifiable diseases, such as Norovirus, or bird flu, can give rise to significant business interruption that would not be covered by the policy wording.

With regards to notifiable disease, the standard Association of British Insurers (ABI) wording refers to *'any human infectious or human contagious disease'* (excluding Aids) rather than disease in any form. This distinction became important following the outbreak of 'mad cow' disease in the recent past, which was a notifiable disease, but not one that related to humans. Not all policy wordings followed the ABI standard, and some policies inadvertently gave cover for claims arising from an outbreak of a notifiable disease affecting animals.

In the majority of cases no business interruption loss could be claimed, as the losses arising did not derive from the outbreak of a notifiable disease a few miles from a particular restaurant, but rather from the fact that customers were largely avoiding rural areas, as invited to do at the time by the authorities.

The Maximum Indemnity Period can be defined by the insured business. In respect of the four aspects of cover listed above, commencement of that period is explicitly set out. It will commence once any notifiable disease has been discovered or a murder/suicide has occurred. The cover in respect of vermin and problems with the drains allows for the indemnity period to commence when restrictions imposed by a local authority come into force.

On one occasion, a business imported significant quantities of nuts and other products on a fair trade basis, from the third world, for repackaging for charity and health food shops. There was a significant infestation of moths, the eggs and larvae of which were inadvertently included with the raw material. The time taken to eradicate all of the hatched moths which had spread throughout the Premises, and the subsequently laid eggs, was significant, as was the amount of physical spoilage. Notwithstanding that the latter was not insured (the action of moths/insects/vermin will be commonly excluded from stock covers), the support of insurers in respect of the business interruption claim was critical to the survival of the business.

With regards to the sanitary arrangements/drains, blockages would not comprise accidents - specific extraneous incidents must occur. In many cases, accidental damage to drains is repairable reasonably quickly and the duty to mitigate loss applies as with any other cover. Again, this is a business interruption extension and the cost of repairing the damage would not, therefore, fall for consideration.

Attempted Murder/Suicide

Murder/suicide at the Premises can give rise to a significant reduction in the level of turnover, where this produces a disinclination for other guests to stay at a hotel, for example. Certain hotels see reasonably high levels of suicide, selected on the basis that they can be relied upon to deal with the matter in a dignified and discreet way.

Two issues are worth raising. Firstly, the definition of Premises is important. A claim was brought on one occasion by a bakery concession in a cut price supermarket. Without any prior warning, one of the employees of the supermarket attacked a number of customers and colleagues with a machete. Some two months later one of the customers that had been badly injured died, and there was understandably a depression in turnover in the immediate aftermath, causing significant cash flow hardship to the concession.

The initial consideration was the definition of Premises - did these comprise merely the area occupied by the concession or the whole supermarket? It was decided that the Premises related to the whole demised building, although that conclusion was not inevitable at the time. The uncertainty that arose whilst the matter was resolved was unsettling for the insured business. Clarification of the definition of Premises in advance would have assisted.

Secondly, the cover specifically relates to murder or suicide. Continuing the example quoted above, when the case of the machete wielding employee went to trial, because the mental health of the individual was deemed to be poor, and it was not considered that he fully understood what he was doing, he was found guilty of manslaughter on the basis of diminished responsibility.

This conclusion of the court was not available for a significant period after the bakery concession claim was concluded. Manslaughter is not an incident triggering cover and consideration was given to the recovery of funds from the insured person which initially were released on the assumption of murder. No action aimed at securing repayment was ultimately taken, but it emphasises that there might be uncertainty as to whether an event constitutes murder or not. The confirmation of an indemnity under this extension can be significantly delayed pending police investigation and the insured business must be prepared to fulfil its obligation to mitigate loss in the interim.

On one occasion, following multiple deaths at a site following an explosion, the police and Health and Safety Executive maintained control over the premises for several months. Insurers eventually had to take legal action to secure access.

Loss of Licence/Franchise

There are a variety of different covers available under this broad heading, the commercial wordings varying significantly.

Following significant damage to a tenanted public house, the brewery (or relevant building owner) may decide not to reinstate the damage but to sell the premises on. They may decide to alter the use of the building, for example, introducing restaurant facilities where none existed before. They may reinstate a public house, but one with significantly different décor and aiming for a significantly different market than before, perhaps with an aspiration to alter the tenant.

This places the insured tenant in a very difficult position. Assuming that an adequate core business interruption policy has been arranged, any loss of profit during the Maximum Indemnity Period will be covered. Tenants will often live above the public house that they manage and their need to attend to their personal situation and the domestic insurance claim alongside the commercial business is a significant issue.

The tenant in this position is likely to have even less control over the building repair programme that would normally be the case - restaurants, clubs and bars will be more sensitive to changing moods and fashions in terms of fixtures and fittings, even more than a retailer (fashion changes will initially impact on stock ranges for them). The possibility of an extended period of down time presents itself whilst all options are considered.

These covers, therefore, anticipate that trading may not have recommenced by the end of the Maximum Indemnity Period and that there may be ongoing loss. In a departure from the normal situation where only losses within the Maximum Indemnity Period will be considered, the loss of licence wordings allow for the value of the lost licence beyond the end of the Maximum Indemnity Period.

It is not the intention of this book to discuss how such future loss might be valued but certain issues involved are obvious. If there is a long license period left to run, that, by definition, will have a greater value than a short period. There is additionally the issue of what the tenant publican will do into the future. Were he to secure an alternative licence arrangement then he will be in a position to generate income that would not have been generated had he continued at the damaged premises. Whilst the Alternative Trading clause explicitly refers to alternative trading within the Maximum Indemnity Period, the principle of indemnity would apply. It would be equitable to acknowledge any new sources of income that would not have been earned but for the operation of an insured peril in calculating any settlement.

There are a wider variety of issues to consider in calculating such ongoing loss compared to trading losses within a fixed period and there is the issue of what else the insured person is doing into the future. As a consequence, these claims might not be resolvable until some time after an incident, and cash flow hardship may result. This is an unavoidable consequence of all relevant factors having to be considered. An awareness that interim payments that might be made during the life of a normal business interruption policy within the Maximum Indemnity Period could be more difficult to make prior to resolution of a loss of licence claim can avoid expectation difficulties.

Franchisees face similar if not identical problems.

In the case of fast food outlets, many franchisees will own all of the assets generating sales and will, therefore, be in control of the repair period. Even so, there may be restrictions in franchise agreements that require stringent performance and which may not allow undue delay in sourcing replacement quotations. This is likely to place particular pressure on material damage sums insured (marginal underinsurance might otherwise be addressed by a longer tendering period). Involuntary betterment might arise by having to comply with ongoing franchisor specification improvements, producing additional pressure on the resources of the insured business. It might be the case, however, that the franchise agreement allows the franchisor a terminal option if there is a cessation of supply for stipulated periods. In considering the need for any extension to the basic cover, the franchise agreement should be carefully considered to identify any such issues.

It will be appreciated that the franchisee who does not own all of the assets is at greater risk following significant damage in the same way as a tenant publican.

Franchisees who form part of a national network may require to carry on making payments to a franchisor regardless of Damage. If such costs have been (incorrectly) uninsured, then a shortfall on settlement will arise. A national network might be reluctant to allow an absence of coverage in significant franchise areas for any period of time, and it would be unusual for there to be no clause within the franchise agreement dealing with this.

These situations refer to businesses which primarily trade through a particular brand or licence. There are, in addition to that, situations where businesses are licensed to produce products for specific points in time. Consider the production of toys and other accessories alongside Hollywood blockbusters. A loss suffered by those businesses would be most appropriately dealt with by a standard business interruption cover with a suitably long Maximum Indemnity Period (and significant Additional Increase in Cost of Working cover).

Underwriters, of course, should be advised if parts of the business are dependent upon delivery of product for specific licences. The destruction of film specific stock or of development work, aimed at producing the same, will likely produce a reduction in turnover within the Maximum Indemnity Period and this will be dealt with through the core cover.

The existence and availability of this type of insurance recognises that licence holders or franchisees are at risk of not having long-term participation in the brand which underpins their business. The much stronger hand in post loss decision making is likely to rest with the brewery, franchisor or other relevant business.

For a normal commercial business which has created its own brand, it would not be appropriate to provide cover for ongoing losses after the end of the Maximum Indemnity Period on the basis that such businesses do have the opportunity to mitigate losses and to directly control the mitigation strategy. As they have the ability to do so, it is equitable that they should carry the risk of success or failure.

Business interruption insurance concerns itself with pecuniary loss rather than inconvenience and a general compensation payment for the future would be inconsistent with that. A normal commercial business which has more direct control over its own destiny is able to protect itself through the selection of an appropriately long Maximum Indemnity Period. Whilst there is increasing focus on brand damage and ongoing tarnishment to reputation, brand damage at the end of the day reveals itself in reduced sales.

There are two final observations to make. Firstly, a franchisee will be required under any of the relevant wordings to demonstrate that every possible effort has been made to mitigate the loss arising and to secure an ongoing licence/franchise to mitigate a loss as would normally be expected. Any failure to do so will invalidate a claim under this head of cover. There is a need to work very closely with the insurer/loss adjuster so that difficulties are identified at the earliest possible time and to give everybody an opportunity of influencing the outcome is essential.

Secondly, it may be that the franchisor will arrange insurance cover for the convenience of franchisees generally, and also so that he knows that they are adequately insured and have not overlooked the need to set-up relevant policies. Whilst such support may be very welcome, it is in the franchisor's interest to ensure that such appropriate policies are taken out. Inevitably, care will have been taken to ensure that primarily his position is protected rather than necessarily taking the position of the franchisee into consideration in the first instance. The appropriateness of such cover should be carefully considered with this in mind.

Contingency Covers

There are certain businesses, notably including those which organise annual trade shows or events, that may not own the building in which their exhibition is to take place but which are at risk of something occurring either there or elsewhere which would provide a disinclination for the public to visit.

Whilst it would be possible to consider altering the standard wording to provide cover following Damage at the exhibition location, the threat to income, which significantly presents itself off site, would still remain. This risk primarily relates to attendance by the public. Trade attendance, where there is a business imperative involved, is less at risk.

A contingency cover acknowledges this and allows for the occurrence of events (undefined) which caused significant number of attendees in the light of such an event to not take part in the exhibition/show. Attendance fees would drop and there could be a significant loss of income.

The requirement (wordings vary) will be for widespread impact of an event not necessarily in one specific region but relating to the United Kingdom generally. Examples would include the stationing of the military around a major airport, a major rail disaster, air crash or some similar occurrence. Strike action, or the deliberate act of any supply undertaking, will often be exclusions, albeit not universally so.

There can be difficulties in establishing quantum where there are large annual events particularly if there is significant variation in the financial results historically. Similar observations apply to those made in respect of Advanced Profits cover above. The extent to which the Gross Profit or Revenue that the cover is being arranged to protect can be audited is a significant issue. If an insured business is unable to at least provide detailed budgets, supplying further supporting documentation if required, this will speak to the ease with which quantum can be demonstrated if a claim were to be made.

Businesses become agitated if a budget was accepted at face value for the calculation of premium, but is considered insufficient to support quantum when a claim is made. The perception is unreasonable - insurers cannot bear the cost of investigating budgets and forecasts regardless of claims arising, as that would have to be reflected in the premium.

It has been the case in the past that, with insurers approval, loss adjusters have investigated quantum in advance of any claim, and have confirmed the reasonableness of budgets (or otherwise) with the cost of them so doing paid by the client. This can be accompanied by an agreement that the element of the loss adjuster's costs that would have been required when a claim is made will then be dealt with by the insurer, via a repayment to the client.

It is, of course, difficult to suggest to an insured business that further outlays be paid on top of what might be perceived as a significant premium. Notwithstanding that, there are businesses taking out contingency covers that have an extremely low ability to demonstrate and prove quantum should a claim be made. It is suggested that the ability to evidence quantum should be properly considered at the time the policy cover is incepted - if there will be significant difficulty, this should be discussed in some detail beforehand. Insurers can only reasonably be expected to make payments if quantum can be verified. It may be that contingency covers will not be the best way to manage risk if quantum will be unduly subjective.

Whilst the discussion of contingency covers has been framed within the context of exhibitions/events, the range of incidences that such cover might be relevant to is very wide. Related cover, for example, deals with non-appearance or cancellation of celebrity attendance at events. In those cases where the cover deals with reimbursement of the cost involved and where the costs can be separately identified, then a lot of the difficulties anticipated in the preceding paragraphs will not arise. Regardless of the precise nature of the contingency, the ability to evidence loss were a claim to be made will often help dictate how the cover is incepted and designed.

A specific type of contingency cover is pluvius insurance, which allows for claims typically on a cost rather than profit/revenue basis to be reclaimed if rainfall cancels an event. The policy will specify precisely the depth of rainfall required over a given period, albeit the depth of rainfall will not always be the most relevant factor.

In respect on motor racing, any rainfall on the track may require suspension of racing (depending on the type of event). Evaporation will clear such moisture differently at different times of the year and the period of time that race marshals disallow racing would be a more relevant reference point than any particular intensity or depth of rain. These are illustrative of the practical issues that can present themselves if a claim is made. The probability of such difficulties arising as an unwelcome surprise can be minimised if the nature of the business is discussed in detail at inception.

There can be difficulty in applying those covers which settle claims on the basis of cost rather than profit or revenue. In the vast majority of cases, the cost of putting on an event, from a village fête to a major sporting event, will be fixed. To the extent that part of the whole of the event cannot be run, those costs relating to that part or the event will have been wasted. The policy reimburses historically incurred, but wasted, costs rather than additional costs to avoid loss.

It can be the case, depending upon the precise circumstances that, after repayment of such costs, the event makes a greater profit than would have been the case if the event had not occurred, albeit the corollary can be true. If most of the revenue is secured by visitors attending in the morning, but costs accrue evenly through the day, then an early afternoon incident will leave the function better off than planned. Whilst the profit may not be the item insured, it is merely noted that an event might ultimately be significantly better or worse off after receipt of insurance monies, which at face value would not represent indemnity. This is unavoidable and is not a problem if the insured person in particular understands the mechanics on how quantum will be addressed in advance.

Of course, the vast majority of events seeking pluvius insurance cover will not be large enough to merit any detailed discussion - the amount at risk will require a commercial approach.

Alien Abduction etc.

It has been said in the past that almost anything can be insured as long as it is fortuitous, and for an appropriate premium. It has been possible to buy policies in respect of the risk of abduction by aliens among other things. The wide range of more esoteric covers, even so far as they indirectly relate to business interruption, will not be discussed in this book due to the low incidence of applicability. In some cases, it might be better to consider placing a bet with a bookmaker rather than attempting to arrange an unusual extension to the core policy where a particular risk is identified. To satisfy Corporate Governance requirements, mere consideration of a risk, with a conclusion that it cannot economically be dealt with, is sufficient for the directors of the business to discharge their duties.

At the Battle of Waterloo, Marshall Blucher, the Prussian General, believed that he had become pregnant by an elephant. Had he been in charge of the risk programme for the Prussian military, he might have considered the risk of pregnancy to the officer class generally (perhaps by a variety of mammals) to be a significant concern and might have commenced relevant discussion with his broker. His view of the risks that life presents may be extreme but he maintained high rank in his day. The expectation gap in terms of what a business interruption policy is capable of delivering needs to be managed.

The fact that it is difficult to consider many more extensions that would in real life be of practical use is a compliment to the core policy wording. Whilst the wording is often criticised as being too generic, that is its virtue not its vice. That there are relatively few extensions that need to be considered confirms that.

7. Clauses Clarifying the Core Cover

There are a number of clauses and covers that apply to commercial policies whether explicitly stated on the face of the policy or not. Such clauses are essentially confirming (existing) aspects of indemnity, and are, therefore, not extending the cover, but they nevertheless provide reassurance to the insured business with regards the policy response in specific situations.

The main clauses falling into this category are set out below.

Other Circumstances

In defining the business interruption cover, most policies will define the terms Rate of Gross Profit, Annual Turnover and Standard Turnover to the left-hand side of one of the pages in the policy, with a large bracket relating these three definitions to a paragraph to the right. That paragraph will essentially allow for any of the three terms to be varied as necessary such that the anticipated financial result most closely resembles what would have occurred but for the incident. Whilst that paragraph has no formal title, it is referred to as the other circumstances or any circumstances clause, as it allows for any circumstances generally that would have affected the business but for an incident to be taken into account in calculating loss.

With regards the Rate of Gross Profit, there has been debate as to whether the other circumstances clause allows companies to claim specific rates of gross profit for particular segments of their business in the absence of a departmental clause on the face of the policy. There is technical merit in this argument, in that the other circumstances clause relates to the Rate (singular) of Gross Profit rather than Rates (plural) of Gross Profit.

However, the use of rates specific to departments may produce a better quantification of the extent of the loss rather than one overall rate.

Accordingly, the Association of British Insurers accept (as set out in the Recommended Practices, Wordings and Procedures manual) that the other circumstances clause specifically includes the following three clauses, regardless of whether they appear on the face of the policy or not:

- Departmental Clause
- New Business Clause
- Salvage Sale Clause

The cover normally available under those clauses is not extended. There are limitations in respect of the application of those clauses and such limitations would apply just as much if they are imported by the other circumstances clause as if they were printed on the face of the policy itself.

Alternative Trading

The alternative trading clause stipulates that, if any turnover that would have been generated from the Premises which suffer an incident, has been generated elsewhere, then such turnover generated elsewhere will be treated as actual turnover in calculating any shortfall payable by the policy.

It is useful to clarify this point, as the policy will only deal with loss at the Premises and there has been much discussion previously in this book with regards to the fact that cover will be related to the Premises rather than anywhere else in most circumstances. The addition of the alternative trading clause avoids an insured business mistakenly assuming that actual turnover generated elsewhere might, therefore, be omitted from the calculations of loss. Most insured businesses will accept that additional turnover generated elsewhere, which would not have been generated but for the incident, should be deducted from anticipated turnover in calculating a loss, in the same way as actual turnover generated normally.

It is tempting to think of the application of the alternative trading clause in terms of a business relocating to brand new premises after the occurrence of an incident. That is not the only situation where the alternative trading clause could apply. If a business has a number of depots, it may be possible to redirect business to one of the other depots or to service customers therefrom at an Increased Cost. Increased turnover at other existing premises is, therefore, also brought within the ambit of the cover.

In the past, following a fire at a leisure multiplex, attempts were made by the insured business to provide coaches to transport customers (free of charge and with free drinks and snacks on-board) to another location that it also owned. The turnover generated from that (which was obviously depressed from what it would have been had there been no incident) was properly brought into the loss calculation, the extra cost of the transport also being dealt with as a mitigation expense, i.e. Increased Cost of Working. The transference of staff to other locations post incident will be suggestive of higher turnover there and will require those other locations to be looked at. Chains of high street stores or restaurants may also benefit from customers transferring their business to other connected shops irrespective of the provision of any incentive for them to do so on the part of the insured business. There will be a need, therefore, to consider the performance (reflected in the turnover figures) of nearby unaffected branches as well as that affected by the incident.

This approach can entail some (unavoidable) delay when a claim is submitted, as well as dissatisfaction if not discussed and planned beforehand. It is useful for the insured business to appreciate that benchmarking between branches, should a claim be made, would be an appropriate activity to undertake. If average monthly turnover over the months prior to an incident is used as the measure of a shortfall at a particular location that has suffered an incident, then a consistent basis of measurement to identify any performance elsewhere is equitable.

New Business

The new business clause acknowledges that the standard wording will not be applicable to a business that does not have a trading history. It will be recalled that Standard Turnover is defined as the turnover in the preceding year over the period which corresponds with the indemnity period post incident. In other words, an incident occurring in February 2004 which affected a business for February, March and April would have a standard turnover initially based on the period February to April inclusive in 2003.

If a business only commenced trading at the beginning of January 2004, then the turnover in the preceding year will be £Nil - it did not exist. To avoid anybody concluding that Standard Turnover should be taken as £Nil (and that there is, therefore, no loss), the New Business Clause clarifies the equitable position, which is that best estimates will be made to establish what the turnover would have been but for the incident.

In practice, many businesses will rely on new finance at inception and a business plan may have been prepared to support such borrowing which would act as an initial starting point in estimating what would have occurred but for the incident. Hopefully, that same business plan will have been used as a basis for calculating the insurable gross profit for policy declaration purposes. Difficulties can arise if the documentation submitted to support a claim is inconsistent with that used to calculate the insurable amount at inception/renewal.

Of course, the existence of a business plan reflects anticipation and is not a guarantee that what was anticipated would have come to pass. This can be augmented by any production plans that may be available and there is likely to be some actual trading history (albeit over a short period) which may speak to the accuracy of the forecast. Alternatively, it may be that a history of forecasting in respect of other businesses (were it to be a group policy, for example) could assist.

The extent to which expenses have been incurred is again an indicator of the turnover anticipation. In the case of a restaurant, the physical number of covers and the number of staff retained to service those covers may allow the reasonableness of revenue to be considered with some accuracy. There will be a physical limit to the number of tables/covers that will fit in the Premises. There have been cases in the past where the suggested level of anticipated income would have entailed waiters working at such speed, and with such dexterity, that the business would perhaps have had to recruit a nurse rather than more waiting staff to cope with the resulting stress and injury that would have been inevitable.

On another occasion, a back street garage carrying out MOT and repair work suggested a level of turnover, following a fire a few months after opening, that would have involved customers queuing around the block to get on to the MOT ramp twenty-four hours per day, seven days per week, 365 days per year. Good mechanics may be in demand, but that claim stretched credulity somewhat.

No special action is required in respect of the new business clause - it is a clarification of the reality of working with what evidence exists if an incident occurs shortly after opening. Notwithstanding that, the onus to prove and quantify a loss remains with the insured business.

Professional Accountants

Many policies automatically include a professional accountants clause. This clause will be of particular assistance to an insured with limited resource in the administration and finance departments.

The professional accountants clause caters for requests from insurers for further documentation and analysis necessary to allow proper consideration of a claim, by providing cover for the costs charged by professional accountants to produce such information.

The cover only relates to further work requested in writing by insurers or their representatives (generally loss adjusters) and would not cover costs arising from work which accountants of an insured business thought would be a good idea at their own initiative.

Likewise, this clause does not provide any cover for the initial calculation of a claim and relates to further information required by insurers. The policy will explicitly confirm that the insured have to submit a claim at their own expense. They can of course be assisted by their accountants in that process, but the costs thereof would not be covered.

To avoid confusion, where the accountants are retained to do work, as well clearly setting out the scope of the exercise in writing, it is a good idea to ask the accountants to provide an indicative budget and to provide an early opportunity for review if the cost of the exercise proves to exceed that budget. Avoidable complications arise where budget indications are given, the work is done and very significantly higher costs are then submitted to the business as a fait accompli.

A further point to appreciate is that this cover does not allow any random firm of accountants to be used, but will relate to the accountants acting regularly for the insured business prior to the incident. A business using the services of a local bookkeeper would not be at liberty to involve one of the large firms of chartered accountants as a special matter for the insurance claim. On the other hand, if one of the large firms of accountants work for the insured business as a matter of course, then it is quite reasonable to allow them to also use that firm for the analysis required.

The cost of the work undertaken by the accountant should reflect the fee structure normally applying to work done for the insured business. Special rates for the claim are inappropriate.

This cover is not intended to pay for the production of information which is readily available to the insured business. For example, a request for a schedule of turnover by month over three years prior to an incident reflects a request for information readily available to the insured business. Mindful of the common law and policy duty to mitigate loss, there will be no need to incur third party accountants costs in producing such basic information. Existing employees will be able to do it. The clause provides support from insurers where extensive further work is required over and above the calculation and submission of the claim initially.

Having required the production of information, in the absence of evidence questioning its integrity, it can be accepted without the need to audit it.

Accounts Designation

The accounts designation clause again is a clarification of the principle of indemnity. Essentially, insurers confirm that they will accept the designation and classification of costs and expenses normally used in the accounts of the insured business for policy purposes.

This can arise as an issue with regard to the definition of Purchases. Consider a situation where company 'A' orders a painted metal bar from a supplier for which it pays £100. Company 'B' may order an unpainted metal bar for £80, asking the supplier to deliver it not to the factory gate but to a subcontract painter in the first instance. The painter paints the bar, for which he charges £20, and then delivers a painted bar to the business which is identical in all physical respects to the painted metal bar received by company 'A'.

Is the purchase cost for company 'B' £100 or £80? The answer will depend on the classification of the costs in the accounts. In the detailed profit and loss account, either there will be a separate expense line for subcontract expenditure (the £20) or alternatively that will be combined and shown within Purchases. This will establish the extent of uninsured costs, and consequently the adequacy of the gross profit declaration. It will also provide the relevant Rate of Gross Profit to apply to any reduction in turnover.

In the case of purchases, if a declaration linked policy has been arranged, then inadvertent underinsurance is avoided albeit the dangers of a fundamentally low declaration remain.

The accounts designation clause, it should be noted, will not assist where the accounts are silent in respect of assets or income streams. Consider heat treatment or chemical treatment businesses that will maintain tanks and baths of various solutions which will simply be topped-up over time as required. The cost of the material added will almost certainly be expensed to the profit and loss account rather than reflected on the balance sheet. In all likelihood it will be dealt with either as purchases or as consumable expenses.

Difficulties will not relate to the accounts designation - that will be a matter of fact. Any difficulty will relate to the adequacy of the stock sum insured if no allowance has been made for the cost involved (which will not appear on the balance sheet) when setting the sum insured. For a large business, six figure sums might be involved. Where such costs have simply been written-off on a year by year basis, the material damage sums insured, and specifically the stock sum insured, may not be adequate to include these items.

This is only one example of an asset that may not present itself on the face of the profit and loss account, and which is an issue as much for the material damage policy as for the business interruption.

Accumulated Stocks

The accumulated stocks clause anticipates a situation where a manufacturing business depletes its buffer stockholding to avoid a reduction in turnover and has not had an opportunity to build such buffer stock backup by the end of the Maximum Indemnity Period. If the stock has not been replaced at that point then the risk of an uninsured loss occurring presents itself. Whilst there is a common law duty to mitigate a loss generally, there is no onus on an insured business to mitigate a loss claimable under an insurance policy at the expense of incurring a loss that is not insured. The accumulated stocks clause anticipates, therefore, not only that there is a risk of loss occurring after the end of the Maximum Indemnity Period but assumes that losses are actually suffered.

In practice, many claims are settled shortly after the end of the Maximum Indemnity Period, if not before. In the majority of cases where there is a depletion of the finished stock, the business is assumed to have suffered loss in that its assets are reduced and there is a risk existent that did not exist prior to the incident, rather than requiring specific evidence of lost turnover. If a business is operating at capacity within normal hours, additional costs such as overtime working are likely to arise to recreate the stock and these are commonly held to satisfy the requirement for financial loss to be suffered.

Without the clarification of this clause, an insured business may find itself in an invidious position. If buffer stock was not depleted to avoid orders being lost, then a failure to mitigate might be a reasonable charge to bring. If the buffer, therefore, is reduced without there being any compensation for the subsequent recreation, then an unintended uninsured loss would arise.

It should be emphasised that this clause relates to undamaged stock which is depleted for the benefit of the business interruption policy rather than damaged stock which will be dealt with under the stock cover. An accumulated stocks payment would be made under the business interruption cover as it represents a cost incurred to avoid a loss of turnover within the defined Maximum Indemnity Period.

In making this last observation it should be emphasised that the depletion of buffer stock which presents potential loss has to arise at the end of the Maximum Indemnity Period and not merely subsist at the end of the actual indemnity period if this is shorter. If additional cost is incurred in building stock backup after the claimed indemnity period but within the Maximum Indemnity Period then the additional cost of remanufacture would be dealt with as an increased cost in the normal manner and the actual indemnity period would be extended.

Finally, there are situations where levels of buffer stock have been reduced after an incident, the business finding that the lower level of buffer remains acceptable. The occurrence of an insured incident causes management to respond to scenarios that would not normally be contemplated. Occasionally, there are strategic beneficial lessons to be gained. In the situation where buffer stock has been reduced and that has avoided a loss of turnover, if there is an intention to maintain the buffer stock at that reduced level, then it would be inappropriate to make a claim under the accumulated stocks clause.

This cover does not represent a compensatory payment relating to the stock reduction, but is rather an indemnity contribution to the cost of recreation. If there is no stock recreation, or if there is no turnover loss demonstrable after the end of the Maximum Indemnity Period directly resulting from the postponement of a turnover loss within the Maximum Indemnity Period via the use of the buffer, then no claim is appropriate.

Departmental

The departmental clause requires that 'if the Business be conducted in different departments, the independent trading results of which are ascertainable' then the business interruption cover will be applied in relation to that department. Typically, on a group basis, each subsidiary will represent a department. Within an individual limited company there may be distinct divisions that run in independently, loss affecting one but not the other(s).

If a particular segment of business is affected by an incident, the loss will most accurately be measured by the financial information relating to that business section rather than to the business overall. If a business sells hens eggs and Fabergé eggs, then the average profitability of the business overall may be significantly different to the profit of a particular department (it will be higher than that of hens eggs, and lower than that of Fabergé).

The application of the departmental clause is not optional. The insured business cannot invoke this clause on a unilateral basis (and commonly when the section of business affected is more profitable than average).

Whilst insurers (or those signing-up to the Association of British Insurers' code) would have no difficulty in a departmental approach being taken, an insured business might be tempted to argue that the policy only allows for an average rate. Setting out an explicit departmental clause on the face of the policy is consequently for the benefit of the policyholder to clarify the fact that more meaningful detailed figures will be utilised in calculating settlement where these are available.

There are businesses that take the concept of the departmental approach to the extreme and seek to claim a specific profit for a transaction or series of transactions. The departmental clause does not provide for this. Inevitably, the section or department of a business will have an average rate of profit which reflects the mix of products sold therein. There is no policy entitlement to adopt a micro approach to the issue of calculation of the Rate of Gross Profit, albeit the agreement of both parties to do so would permit it.

There is no definition of what a 'department' comprises other than requiring that the segment of the business entity to which the term applies should generate independent trading results which are ascertainable. In a manufacturing business products may pass through a variety of processes and the selling price ultimately may be built-up using charge out rates for specific machines. Notwithstanding such notional charge out rates, it would be unlikely for each machine process to be a separate profit centre within the books and records and the departmental approach, therefore, would not allow a period of downtime to be valued in terms of lost turnover by taking the number of hours lost multiplied by the notional charge out rate for the machine. There would be a need to demonstrate a turnover loss for the business segment overall.

Salvage Sale

The salvage sale clause relates to a situation where a business will sell stock damaged by an insured incident (whether smoke, water or impact damage) at a reduced price rather than selling it to salvage dealers. The salvage sale proceeds will invariably be significantly greater than those which a dealer would be able to offer, and the availability of discounted stock would potentially help stimulate customer interest in the business and generate turnover over and above that directly generated by the discounted goods. Customers might purchase undamaged stock (if there is any) at full price when they buy discounted salvage, although there is a danger that the opposite may happen.

The salvage sale may be a one-off event, where all stock available for sale represents salvage, or the salvage may be sold in parcels over a period of time alongside good stock. To some extent, the approach may be dictated by the extent of Damage to the Premises. If there is extensive smoke Damage throughout the building, then it might be advisable to sell-off as much of the smoke damaged stock as possible prior to refurbishment and cleaning being undertaken. Progressive discounts might be offered such that the stock is removed at a point convenient to commencement of general cleaning within the overall mitigation strategy.

The selling price (and, therefore, the Gross Profit earned) in respect of product in a salvage sale will be lower than normal. It is recognised that it is, therefore, unfair to treat it as actual turnover to be credited to the business interruption claim in the normal way. Normally, in calculating a business interruption loss, any Actual Turnover achieved is deducted from Standard Turnover and a payment is made in respect of the Reduction in Turnover at the Rate of Gross Profit from the accounts ended most recently prior to the incident. It is assumed implicitly that both the Standard Turnover and the Actual Turnover generate the same average Rate of Gross Profit. In the case of a salvage sale, such an assumption will not be valid.

To reflect this, and to avoid penalising the insured business, the actual salvage turnover is not deducted from standard turnover in calculating the reduction, albeit any other actual turnover outside the scope of a salvage sale would be. The Rate of Gross Profit is applied to the shortfall in turnover to calculate a loss of Gross Profit (which excludes any adjustment for or inclusion of salvage sale turnover at that point). The Gross Profit generated by the salvage sale is then deducted as a separate item from the previously calculated loss of Gross Profit to provide the loss of Gross Profit to be included in the settlement. By dealing with the salvage profit as a separate item, the insured business is not penalised for the lower level of profitability that a salvage sale will generate.

Difficulty can arise where a stock settlement is being sought in advance of a business interruption settlement. In such a situation, an insured business may make a notional contribution to retain salvage themselves (effectively submitting a blind tender alongside salvage dealers), accepting a lower settlement in respect of stock in return for the right to retain it themselves.

This can distort the subsequent profit in a salvage sale as the cost of the stock for salvage sale purposes will no longer be the historic cost price, but will be restated at the level of the deduction from the stock claim which effectively comprises the price that the insured business has paid to the insurer to retain the stock itself. A subjective assessment has to be made of the value of the affected stock. When it is sold in the salvage sale, the financial loss arising from the stock damage will crystallise via a reduced selling price. If the loss in value of stock which is actually crystallised in the salvage sale is significantly different to the assumption made when the insured business calculated the amount it would be prepared to pay to retain the salvage itself, a distortion can arise.

It is recommended that a stock settlement be left open, therefore, until a salvage sale is completed. At that point, the loss suffered is crystallised and can be apportioned between the business interruption and stock covers objectively, rather than on the basis of assumption.

Avoidable complications arise due to the fact that a depressed selling price on salvage sale is partly a material damage issue and partly a business interruption issue. An insured business may be tempted to argue that if a selling price is reduced from that which would otherwise be expected, but that nevertheless exceeds the historic cost, then the claim solely relates to business interruption rather than stock.

Whilst any material damage excess might thereby be avoided, this is nevertheless not a clever argument. If it is wholly a business interruption issue, then the material damage proviso might not be satisfied and the claim might fail in its entirety. At any rate, the reason that the selling prices have reduced, whether those ultimately achieved remained higher than cost or not, is because of the physical damage suffered. Part of the claim relates to the stock and part to the business interruption. If there is a policy cover difficulty in respect of one of those sections of the policy (stock underinsurance, for example) then the impact of an error in properly apportioning a loss between business interruption and stock could produce hardship. Making an assumption (with regards the correct level of payment to retain the salvage) to settle a stock claim unduly early is likely to court error.

There is no specific requirement to include a salvage sale clause on the face of the policy. The application of the clause will generally be to the benefit of the insured person and there is unlikely to be a complaint if it is introduced. That can contrast with the departmental clause which will not always be to the benefit of the insured business and in respect of which there is a greater need for explicit incorporation.

8. Stock

The Stock/Business Interruption Overlap

Whereas many component parts of the material damage cover, plant and machinery and buildings insurance foremost among them, relate to items appearing on a company's balance sheet, stock is relevant both to the balance sheet and to the profit and loss account.

Taking a typical profit and loss account, the gross profit insurance will provide cover for the gross profit and all of the costs there under. The expenditure deducted in arriving at gross profit from turnover will either be dealt with on the basis that such costs will cease if an insured event occurs (hence the logic of uninsuring them) or, to the extent that such costs relate to stock in hand at the time of the incident, they will be dealt with by the material damage cover.

It follows that the claim for stock plus the associated claim for business interruption (in respect of that stock) cannot exceed turnover - these claims reflect different constituent parts of the selling price, not any amount in excess of it. The insured business cannot be better off after making a claim when it would have been had it not been for the incident.

Consider the following circumstance:

A furniture manufacturer sells a dining table and four chairs with a selling price of £1,000 calculated as follows:

	£
Raw materials (pine)	400
Labour	200
Direct overheads	100
Indirect overheads	200
Net profit	100
	1,000

The dining table and chairs are destroyed and there is no backup stock. An order is lost because the customer shops elsewhere prior to the stock being replaced.

Typically, the material damage claim would be settled first. The insured business will make a claim for stock in accordance with its normal accounting valuation and agrees a settlement of £700 with the stock insurer as follows:

	£
Raw materials (pine)	400
Labour	200
Direct overheads	100
	700

Subsequent to settlement of the stock claim, the business interruption claim is submitted. The insured business may consult the policy wording, and, assuming that only Purchases are uninsured, a claim for £600 is submitted. (£1,000 selling price less £400 Purchase cost.)

The total claim would then total £1,300 as follows:

	£
Material damage	700
Business interruption	600
Direct overheads	1,300

This is anomalous. Had there not been an incident then the business would have received £1,000. It cannot be right as a basic principle of indemnity that an insured business can be better off after an insured incident than it would otherwise have been had such an event not occurred.

The reason that there is a £300 over claim is that the labour and direct overheads, which total £300, have been claimed under the stock item whilst also being insured under gross profit (given that all costs other than Purchases have been insured thereunder). In practice, loss adjusters would simply deduct £300 from the business interruption claim.

Such a pragmatic approach may be acceptable if the same insurer is on risk for the business interruption and material damage, and if the sums insured are adequate. If not, the business interruption insurer would no doubt be delighted to see a reduction in the claim presented to him, but the stock insurer might not share that view.

Sharing the degree of over insurance evenly might be a workable solution - in the example above the business interruption insurer would enjoy a claim reduction of 6/13ths of £300 (£138) which reflects the fact that £600 of the gross £1,300 claim represents the business interruption insurer's independent liability, with the stock insurer seeing a reduction of £162 (£700/£1,300 multiplied by £300).

The revised settlement would then be as follows:

	Initial Claim	Less Duplication	Settlement
	£	£	£
Stock	700	162	538
Business interruption	600	138	462
	1,300	300	1,000

Another simple example of the interface between the stock and the business interruption insurance might assist. Consider a sofa with a normal selling price of £3,000. This sofa costs £1,800 and normal profit generated thereon would be £1,200 representing a Rate of Gross Profit of 40%. Let us suppose that water leaks into the Premises and affects the sofa such that it has to be sold at a reduced price of £2,000. Let us also assume that there is an excess in respect of the material damage policy of £500.

The cash loss to this business would amount to £1,000, being the reduction in cash proceeds received from the customer (£3,000 minus £2,000). The practical difficulty is apportioning that loss between the business interruption and material damage policies. As discussed in respect of salvage sales, there may be a temptation for the insured business to argue that the loss is entirely a business interruption matter given that the actual sale proceeds exceed the cost. Such an approach may also be attractive as it avoids the application of the material damage excess. However, if the loss relates entirely to business interruption rather than to material damage, then no amount may be payable by the insurer as the Material Damage Proviso may not be satisfied. The reason that the selling price is reduced is because of the physical damage.

There is no perfect way to apportion the loss, but a practical suggestion would be to assume that the rate of gross profit normally enjoyed is maintained in achieving the lower selling price. In this case, the reduced gross profit generated might be calculated as 40% of £2,000 which amounts to £800. This is £400 less than the gross profit normally enjoyed, and that would, therefore, represent the business interruption loss.

Of the £1,000 overall loss, therefore, £400 would relate to business interruption. By deduction, the remaining £600 would, therefore, represent the stock loss. From this, the £500 excess needs to be deducted, to give a settlement in respect of stock at £100. The monies received by the insured business will total £500.

The logic of assuming that the Rate of Gross Profit is maintained on the lower selling price actually received is subject to criticism, but some notional assumption has to be made if the loss is to be divided between the material damage and business interruption covers.

Stock Cost Profile

The above examples emphasise the fact that the cost of stock may not comprise raw materials only. The stock costings may also incorporate variable costs (such as the electricity to run the machine to make a widget), and also fixed costs. The latter may include the rates payable to the local authority for the Premises, but also costs such as direct labour (including the core element of overtime) which are also to a large extent fixed.

For the purposes of settling an insurance claim for stock, the inclusion of raw material purchases is non-contentious. A claim for variable costs could be met, albeit it would have to be appreciated that this produces some overlap with the business interruption claim (as illustrated in the previous examples).

Whilst the variable costs could be paid under the stock cover, subject to deduction from the business interruption, that is not the case with fixed costs. Whilst they may be included in a stock valuation for accounting purposes, which is based on historic cost incurred, the insurance policy, reflecting indemnity, will be based upon the costs that will be incurred in the future to put the insured business back in the position that it would have been but for the Damage.

To be clear, the rates bill will still be paid to the local authority whether ten widgets are manufactured or eleven and will not be relevant to that estimation of loss.

In one extreme example, a traditional business manufactured sewing needles for the American craft market, and the workforce hand polished the needles including the inside of the eye. This was labour intensive work such that each pound of cost on the balance sheet comprised one pence raw material, 80 pence labour, and 19 pence overheads. This cost profile only came to light when a claim occurred. The insured business assumed that any stock claim would be based upon the existing cost profile, particularly given that the latter had been used for the basis of making stock declarations to insurers on a regular basis to establish the stock sum insured. There had been no explicit discussion as to how cost was defined in any of the conversations that had taken place between the insured business and the broker or insurer, and difficulty arose at the time of the claim.

The insured business appreciated that it could not claim more than selling price (in respect of the combined stock claim and that element of the business interruption claim relating to it) and that there was a need to deduct at least the labour cost from the business interruption claim.

However, there was subsequent discussion with regards to the premiums that had been paid over a number of years to insure a cost that did not provide any benefit at claims time.

Such a criticism is not necessarily reasonable. Claims relate to fortuitous unforeseen events and the fact that the policy cover responds in a particular way after an incident does not mean that it would respond in that way in every case.

With regards to insuring of variable overheads under the stock and business interruption covers, it should not be assumed that this is necessarily a bad thing. The critical question in considering the matter for the insured business to ask itself is this: can there be a stock loss without there being a corresponding business interruption loss? If the answer is no, and if there will always be a business interruption claim following any stock loss, then there would be no need to include any overheads under the stock item. The only elements that would need be insured as cost in respect of stock should be those items which are deducted from turnover as uninsured working expenses to calculate gross profit in respect of the business interruption cover.

A business may appreciate that such an overlap exists, but, as a conscious decision, elects to insure particular costs under both the material damage and business interruption covers. Of course, that is quite different to the scenario where there has been no previous discussion and the policy response is a surprise at claims time.

There is one proviso that has to be made in respect of the comments set out above with regards the double counting of overhead. Those comments assume that the stock which has been damaged (to be differentiated by depletion of buffer in respect of the Accumulated Stocks Clause) has been remanufactured/replaced by the end of the Maximum Indemnity Period.

If that is the case, then the variable overheads comprising part of the stock valuation will have been incurred prior to the end of the Maximum Indemnity Period and, therefore, will overlap with the business interruption cover. If the damaged stock is not remanufactured/replaced until after the end of the Maximum Indemnity Period, then the overheads will not be incurred until after the expiry of the business interruption cover. The overheads incurred to remanufacture stock will be those of the subsequent financial year. If that is the case, then there may be no overlap between the stock and business interruption covers and both might achieve full recovery in respect of the variable costs claimed.

Standard Costings

Many manufacturing businesses make standard assumptions about the costs that will be incurred to manufacture stock and will refer to such assumptions as Standard Costings.

Under a Standard Costing system, the insured business will estimate how many widgets will be manufactured in a particular period, and will also estimate what the annual expense will be of a variety of costs. The assumed costs are then apportioned evenly over the assumed widgets. If 100 widgets are going to be made, and if the assumed electricity bill is £100, then £1 will be added to each widget in respect of that electricity cost. However, it will be appreciated that these are merely assumptions and that more or fewer widgets could be manufactured or the electricity bill could be higher or lower than expected. If the electricity bill only amounted to £80 for example, the standard costing system would in the first instance erroneously absorb £100 of electricity cost over the year in accordance with the standard assumption.

To rectify this, businesses will tend to include variances in their profit and loss account, which are financial adjustments to reflect the differences between the standard assumptions and the actual experience. The variances may be calculated to various levels of detail and will separately identify any variation in cost due to the fluctuation in the expense category (a price variance) or alternatively to the amount of product obtained from raw material over and above (or below) the standard assumption (the usage variance).

The purpose of raising the matter is not to become too embroiled in a discussion of a standard costing system, but if an insured business uses that valuation approach, it is more likely that a range of overheads will be absorbed into stock, some of which are likely to be fixed, and there may be a resulting need to discuss the stock cost profile in some detail prior to loss arising.

There is no need to become bogged down in accounting detail. The insured business can be directed to consider the extent to which costs are being included in stock over and above the cost captions which are uninsured to calculate gross profit under the business interruption cover. The need for any overlap in insurance and the implication for any potential claim can then be drawn out and discussed.

As a simple example of a standard costing consider the following:

Production of a deluxe cardigan in the "Manor Born" design					
Standard spec.	**Standard weight**	**Waste factor**	**Costing weight**	**Material cost**	**Cost £/sqm**
Yarn	1.305	0.05	1.371	4.87	6.68
Polyprop	1.000	0.10	1.100	0.22	0.24
Lochweave	1.000	0.10	1.100	0.25	0.28
Latex	1.205	0.00	1.205	0.21	0.25
					7.45
Overheads	**Direct**	**Indirect**			
Labour	0.285	N/A			
Variable	0.069	N/A			
Fixed	0.174	0.506			1.03
	Direct	**Indirect**			
Sales & admin	0.05	1.57			
Distribution	0.47	0.08			2.17
					10.65

The above tabulation reflects an actual claim submission received in the past. The four rows at the top relate to the profile and cost of the raw material purchases. The standard weight column relates to the amount of material actually required to make a cardigan. The column to the right of that includes manufacturing wastage such that the column to the right of that represents the amount of raw material to be purchased to allow for such wastage. It is that amount that needs to be costed. If the material cost column represents up-to-date purchase costs which can be compared to invoice, then it may be that the cost of the raw materials in total in the amount of £7.45 is reasonably stated. (Some businesses update standard costings every time invoice details are input into the accounting system, the keying in of the invoice information automatically updating the stock master file. Other businesses are more tardy and there have been examples where these standard costings have not been updated for some years.) There are two further entries in the right-hand column which are added to the £7.45 to produce the unit cost of £10.65.

The first item amounts to £1.03, which is the total of the amounts to the left of that under the columns headed 'direct' and 'indirect'. Direct costs are those relating to a particular production department, whereas indirect costs are attributable to the Premises overall rather than to the specific department and which to some extent are arbitrarily apportioned. Those costs are further subdivided into 'labour', 'variable' and 'fixed'.

Assuming that the description that the insured business has given is accurate, fixed costs will by definition not increase if the number of cardigans re-manufactured after Damage increases. They are, therefore, not relevant to the calculation of an insurance claim albeit accounting standards permit them to be included in a balance sheet valuation for accounting purposes. Assuming that labour costs included in the core element of overtime are also fixed, to all intents and purposes, then the only cost that would be included for the claim settlement would be £0.069 in relation to the variable costs.

With regards to the £2.17 which is also added to provide the claimed cost of £10.65, that relates to sales administration and distribution costs (this is again the total of the columns to the left). Accounting standards do not allow sales costs to be included in a stock valuation. Sometimes, the descriptions of cost categories can be misleading. There are businesses that treat manufacturing sites as complete production departments and which do apportion all of the costs relating thereto in the stock valuation.

Disregarding the technical accountancy aspects of that, it would generally not be the case that sales and administration or general distribution costs will vary according to modest levels of remanufacturing and these costs are likely to be fixed, as proved to be the case with regards to the actual claim that this standard costing related to.

Against the £10.65 claimed, the two acceptable amounts were £7.45 relating to raw material and £0.069 relating to direct variable costs. For convenience, this can be rounded to £7.45.

In essence, the insured business was paying premium on £3.20 (£10.65 minus £7.45) per unit of stock which could never be claimed in the event of an insured event. (Debatably, the labour cost could be paid as stock but there would be no net benefit if that was subsequently deducted from the business interruption claim.) As before, the concern of the insured business might not be that the suggested claim settlement is unreasonable, but rather that premiums have been wasted previously.

In extreme cases, if a very large quantity of stock was destroyed, such that an additional factory, for example, had to be built to deal with the remanufacturing, a lot of the above points might prove to be incorrect - the costs which have been described as fixed would indeed then increase. Stock claims of that magnitude are not common.

The point to be drawn from the previous comments is that **many businesses overinsure stock, unwittingly**.

Cost/Selling Price

There are businesses who may advise, following a stock loss, that there is no capacity internally to re-manufacture and that the only way to replace stock is to purchase it as a commodity on the open market. Fungible assets such as paper clips may fall into this category. Assuming that all competitors in the market place charge a similar price, then if there is a need to purchase product from somebody else rather than re-manufacture in-house, then the amount paid would be similar to the businesses' own selling price. If that will inevitably be the cost incurred after any incident, then it may be appropriate, contrary to everything that has been noted above, for the sum insured to be calculated with reference to selling prices rather than any cost profile.

That situation is to be distinguished from the situation where a business does have some capacity internally, but due to commercial pressure subcontracts externally to protect the business interruption claim. In that case, the additional cost will be claimed under the business interruption cover as an increased cost of working (subject to economics). The suggestion that turnover (selling prices), as opposed to original cost, potentially reflects the loss in respect of stock would only be relevant where there is no opportunity, through a lack of capacity at any point, for re-manufacture to occur internally. In such a situation, the need to contract a third party is not a matter of choice but indeed the only way to replace stock.

It was suggested above that the stock claim cost plus the business interruption claim will in theory always equal selling price and can never exceed it. In reflecting this truism, an agricultural policy will merely pay out the selling price in the first instance without seeking to break that down into an arbitrary stock/business interruption division.

Non-Manufactured Stock

The above comments relate to manufactured stock. Different issues arise in respect of the work in progress in respect of a solicitor or professional accountant, for example. In those cases, there will be no need to separately insure work in progress as the business interruption cover will be written on a Gross Revenue basis. The labour cost that will be incurred in respect of reconstituting audit files, for example, will already be insured under the business interruption cover. Files, of course, may not be considered strictly to be stock but rather documentation, books and records.

The sum insured on books and records selected by many businesses is, generally speaking, far too low. Most professional practices will retain their files for, say, a six year period. There can be a temptation, if one file destroyed has to be recreated, for a code to be set-up on the computer system and for relevant staff to charge their time to that, a claim then being submitted in respect of the hours logged multiplied by the charge out rates (selling prices).

If that were the correct basis to claim, the sum insured for six years worth of working files would amount to six times the annual revenue (at current prices). The cost of technical books and other professional documentation would be in addition to that. In the majority of cases, sums insured on books and records would be thoroughly inadequate, typically around 5% of the amount that would be required if a claim should be met on the basis of selling prices.

In reality, not all files will be recreatable even were there to be a desire to recreate them. In respect of a solicitors practice, there is a significant difference between conveyancing files and litigation files. Litigation files cannot be recreated, or at least not recreated in full, as notes of meetings, telephone conversations and the like may simply be lost. It might be the case that such information is retained on the computer system, but of course if that is the case then there has been no loss - the exposure exists primarily where hard copy documentation is not fully replicated electronically.

This contrasts with conveyancing files. For conveyancing in respect of registered properties, there may be a need to obtain copy documents from the Land Registry, repeat business when the client moves property again otherwise being jeopardised. In the case of unregistered properties (i.e. those that have not legally changed hands prior to inception of the Land Registry), action will definitely need to be taken, including an indemnity being provided to any future purchaser with regards to potential defect in title. This can be dealt with via an indemnity premium extension.

The nature of the files will dictate the extent to which they need to be insured.

Whatever the conclusion, it might be preferable to exclude books and records from the general definition of contents, which will be subject to underinsurance, and insure them separately under a Limit of Indemnity with no average provision.

A final note to make in respect of files completed by professional offices is that these may be stored in an off site archive operated by a third party. It may be that there will be no cover should such files be destroyed as the Damage will not occur at the Premises as defined in the policy. Extension of the material damage cover in respect of books and records to that third party location will be essential. Even if that is done, no business interruption claim could be made as the material damage proviso will not be satisfied unless such off site books and records are insured by an extension of the definition of Premises rather than merely extending the material damage cover.

Conclusion

In practice, difficulties are more likely to be encountered in respect of stock settlements than in respect of business interruption settlements. Ironically, the business interruption policy explicitly states, in respect of the calculation of the Rate of Gross Profit, that opening stock and closing stock should be valued in accordance with the normal accounting principles of the insured business. Whilst this clarification is provided in respect of the basis of stock valuation for business interruption purposes, the stock cover itself provides no such guidance. Insurers undertake to pay the amount of loss or damage, but policies offer no further guidance over and above that. It would be inappropriate to have discussed in some detail the various aspects that might be worthy of consideration in setting a business interruption sum insured only to ignore the issue of stock in the light of this comment, given the interface of stock with business interruption in the profit and loss account.

9. The Brave New World

Overview

The issue of cyber liability (cyber third party) has been well rehearsed in the past, which contrasts with the position of the first person insured. Initially, liability issues were perhaps more overt, the dangers that e-mail posed being highlighted by high profile and occasionally salacious cases, *Morse -v- Future Reality (1996)* being the best example. On that occasion, a man set out, in some detail, in an e-mail, the sexual exploits that he had engaged in with his girlfriend, the male ego getting the better of what should have been a natural sense of caution. Within a short time, the e-mail had been passed (obviously in confidence on each occasion) from one person to another, all around the world. The potential to reach unintended recipients was demonstrated.

The potential danger of e-mail readily presents itself - if I send an e-mail to you which carries a virus which then infects your system and causes you loss, will I be liable to you for those losses?

Of course, for every person sending a virus laden e-mail in a hypothetical scenario, there has to be somebody on the receiving end. From the latter's perspective, it will inevitably be of most concern to understand whether their insurer will provide any support for recovery from the effects of any such virus in the immediate future. The issue of whether it will be possible to sue the third party sending the e-mail (let alone whether the liability insurer of the sender will be involved) is likely to be a secondary issue.

The extent of coverage for first person claims rather than third party liability claims is the primary issue considered here. For convenience, the electronic perils presenting themselves will be referred to as digital risks.

The current position is that many property (material damage and business interruption) insurers would either perceive that they are not providing cover against digital risk, or, alternatively, that this has been comprehensively excluded in their policy wordings. Alongside such commercial combined policies, specific policies offering virus/hacking cover have appeared over the last couple of years. The take-up of such additional policies at the current time is not extensive.

It is not the place of this book to consider how real the threat of viruses/hacking really is. There are reports that overt hacking losses exceed half a billion pounds per annum, and that over 70% of businesses have suffered a hacking attack with an average cost of £100,000. Unfortunately, the very large figures bandied around are based on estimates and extrapolations and are almost impossible to verify or audit. Likewise, the suggested cost of hacking attacks generally includes apportionment of management time and other fixed overheads rather than additional cash costs. It seems unlikely that over 70% of businesses can have suffered incidents costing them more than £100,000 without the newspapers and television screens being devoted to the topic, which they are not.

Additionally, there will be suspicion that the IT industry is talking the matter up given the experience of the Year 2000 and the millennium bug.

Unfortunately, as even those of us have been on the receiving end of viruses on personal computers at home can confirm, their impact can be very significant. Most businesses benefit from the use of both firewalls and virus protection software in recognition of this.

When it comes to the insurance position with regards such risks, there can be a difficulty generating significant levels of (pre claim) interest. Detailed aspects of IT may not be sexy enough to generate interest at executive level, and insurance, whilst essential, is likewise not a source of fascination for many purchasers.

A consequence of not having considered this matter in any particular detail is that assumption, referred to on many occasions previously in this book, will reveal itself only at claims time. A business might own an advertising hoarding at a sports ground and might also have an electronic advertisement on the World Wide Web. In the absence of detailed discussion, is it reasonable for the businessman to assume that the insurance policy will deal with one in a fundamentally different way to the other? If there has been detailed discussion with the insurance broker with regards the physical advertisement, to what extent will the insured businessman appreciate silence (or what will he infer from it) in respect of the digital advertisement?

Categories of Exposure

It is worth setting out the various ways in which a business may be exposed to digital risk. There can be a danger that, if a business is not actually trading on the Internet, then digital risk will be deemed of low importance, and in many cases this is probably fair. Exposure can be created whether a business is trading on the Internet or not.

Digital activity on the part of a business might be broadly categorised under the following four captions:

1. Electronic Trading

Full-blown trading across the Internet carries obvious risks. The possibility of site security being breached, or the whole website being duplicated by a hoaxer, or of payment details being intercepted and diverted, all present themselves. However, in all likelihood, a business that has decided to start trading across the Web will have had to have explicitly considered security issues, and electronic trading, therefore, may present less of a risk than the other three areas noted below.

Reference to Internet trading often suggests the image of businesses selling items to customers. Exposures can, of course, also arise where purchasing is being carried out electronically, at a consumable level such as stationery reordering as well as the bulk purchase of standard raw materials. The former might be termed convenience purchasing which might not be high profile enough to attract the same level of attention to security and control as the latter.

2. Advertising

There are businesses that have websites that are intended as virtual advertising hoardings or catalogues, rather than interactive trading portals. Websites can be hacked into and defaced. Various political parties can testify to this, as can electronically available periodicals. On one agricultural website, a survey had been posted purporting to set out what activities farmers like to engage in with their livestock. The content clearly identified it as an unauthorised addition.

The websites of commercial enterprises may also suffer electronic vandalism/graffiti, as may charities. On one occasion, a private, non-profit making boarding school failed to notice the addition to its website of the details of an initiation ceremony for new pupils that the headmistress was alleged to offer.

3. E-mail

E-mail activity can inadvertently send and receive viruses, albeit the observance of proper protocols by staff can minimise this risk, alongside firewalls and protection software.

4. Other Internet Activities

There are many reasons why employees would be on the Internet (for valid reasons) which are not captured under the above headings. Insurers and insurance brokers might use the Internet to search for future prospects (as might business development departments in a whole range of businesses), or software upgrades might be downloaded for computerised plant and equipment. Downloading upgrades is now the norm compared to even the recent past, when a floppy disk or CD-Rom containing a software patch would be received through the post.

The above categorisation emphasises the fact that almost all businesses will have some form of exposure to digital risk. The issue, and consequently the availability of insurance cover (if that represents the appropriate risk management response) is not a matter solely for FTSE 100 companies, but for all.

As a postscript, alongside all of the above valid reasons why employees might be on the Internet, it has been suggested that over 70% of employee time on the Internet is spent surfing porn sites. Whilst it is difficult to believe that employees have that amount of spare time on their hands, image filtering software employed in many professional businesses has been found to detect significant numbers of e-mails with inappropriate content.

The Operative Clause

Catastrophic financial loss is more likely to manifest itself in business interruption rather than material damage claims. In the long-term, it is likely that lower and lower levels of capital investment will be necessary to achieve significant levels of turnover This is illustrated by the significant number of individuals running £1 million turnover businesses on the Internet from their homes, as opposed to building factories to achieve the same result. Lower material damage exposures may accompany higher business interruption risk. (This suggested trend is conjectural. Over the last four years, business interruption claims have not increased in proportion to material damage.)

It is worth revisiting the operative clause in respect of the business interruption cover which will require the operation of an insured peril, which is not otherwise excluded, impacting upon property owned or used by the business at the Premises.

If there is Damage to such property, then the Material Damage Proviso is going to be satisfied and (assuming that loss flows from the Damage) a business interruption claim can be submitted. However, various key questions present themselves for consideration.

What Constitutes Premises?

It was noted previously that Premises tend not to be defined in policy wordings, but reference is usually made to the Premises listed on the schedule. When many wordings were written, the notion that Premises could be anything other than a physical location would not have been contemplated. However, there is now the question of whether a website comprises Premises or not. Of course, it cannot be the insurer's intention for Premises to embrace something not in contemplation at inception, and it would seem a pragmatic suggestion for the broker and insurer to consider the appropriateness of adding the website to the list of Premises if it is agreed that the protection of an insurance policy is the best way to manage digital risk.

There is the further question of where the website is. If this is hosted by a third party Internet service provider, then it may not be at the existing Premises on the schedule. If a business hosts its own website, the server supporting the site may exist at the Premises already listed on the schedule, no further specific amendment being necessary. However, it could be queried as to whether a website, as a discreet location exists. Some advanced websites configure themselves from component elements according to the user profile, and, in one sense, the website viewed by a particular user may not, therefore, exist prior to them entering it.

A parallel may be drawn with the Gotham City spotlight used to project an image of a bat on to the clouds to alert batman to the fact that the city needs his assistance. One might question whether the bat image exists on the cloud or on the projector. If it exists on the projector then that will make it more likely for websites hosted by a business itself (at the Premises listed on the schedule) to fall within the scope of cover.

An issue arose in the past with regards to one of the well-known Internet search engines, where a client was seeking to trace Nazi memorabilia. Different national jurisdictions take different stances in respect of such issues. A website was hosted in one jurisdiction, but was accessible from many others. The question arose as to where the website was actually located and which jurisdiction applied. This necessitated consideration of where a website's boundaries end, a matter resolved (usually) more easily with tangible realty.

In amplifying this point, it may be useful to consider a hypothetical website offering all manner of services to allow the public to host parties. A hyperlink button from the party website may take the user to the website of a firework provider to make the party go with a bang. It may or may not be obvious to the user that a different website has been entered. The contractual position between the parties in the case of an accident is one issue. The lack of preciseness in defining the boundaries between websites (whether it has been considered a virtue on the part of the authors of those sites to maximise seamless transition) will affect both this issue and many others. Where it is the intention of a policy to provide some coverage for a website as Premises, the scope of such cover might prove to be more extensive (as a result of difficulty in drawing boundaries) than anticipated unless couched with appropriate wordings.

Having considered the issue of Premises, there is then the matter of property.

Damage to Software
The key issue here is whether software damage should be equated to Damage to material property, thereby satisfying the material damage proviso.

Policy wordings are a little more explicit in this respect than is the case with Premises. With regards the definition of all other contents in the Association of British Insurers' (ABI) recommended wording (which many policies follow), it is noted that the term 'Contents' excludes... *'[costs incurred in respect of]...(E) computer systems and records except for an amount not exceeding £X in respect of the cost of materials and of clerical labour and computer time expended in producing such records'*.

The intention of this item is to exclude business interruption losses from this part of the policy. That is not to the detriment of the insured business - labour costs, along with all other operative expenses, would be dealt with under the business interruption cover if they were either additional or if they gave rise to a loss of gross profit (consequent upon a reduction in turnover). The intention is to avoid any misunderstanding that such costs will be covered under both sections of the policy.

Ironically, in excluding consequential losses, the cost of materials and labour in producing such records may be specifically included. It is difficult to conclude that 'computer systems and records' will not include software, and in that respect, the policy wording, in attempting to exclude something for clarity may be explicitly confirming that software damage does represent material damage.

There could be a debate as to whether the manner of affixation of data to the underlying storage medium is relevant or not. Categorisation of physical assets between buildings and contents is dependent in part upon the manner and degree of affixation. Software irrevocably saved on a storage device might be viewed differently to software which is temporarily stored pending future overwriting.

In addition to the policy wording, there is the precedent of insurers having paid for the loss of dongled software for many years. A dongle is either a physical or electronic lock which ensures that a particular software package will only operate on a specific piece of hardware. Such dongles are of use in industry sectors where software packages can cost many multiples of the price of the basic hardware, and are intended to discourage software piracy or copying of programmes over and above any licence agreement.

If a personal computer is stolen (with a value of perhaps £1,000) but had loaded on it a £30,000 CadCam design software package, then the software supplier will often require a new copy of the software to be purchased to avoid the possibility of staged theft and the sacrifice of a modestly priced piece of hardware in exchange for a further copy of the expensive software. The majority of insurers have been paying for the replacement of such dongled software for many years.

The historical precedent and the policy wording confirms software damage as material damage and opens the way for subsequent material damage and business interruption claims.

What is Damage?

It was previously noted that Damage is a term which, although defined as 'loss or damage', lacks particular clarity. Virus or hacking affected software which is not functioning, either at all, or with the normal efficacy, may be accepted as being damaged. At the current time, the law in the United Kingdom has not considered the specific issue of whether loss of software or computer code (with no other concurrent damage) constitutes Damage or not.

The issue of theft is slightly different. In the majority of cases business will have efficient backup processes such that the last backup can be reloaded (subject to the comments made in respect of dongled software above). If that is the case, then the definition of theft per the Theft Act 1968, i.e. permanent deprival of the use of an asset, might not be satisfied. What a business will have lost is unique enjoyment of the asset, which may be reflective of a crime having taken place, but not one that necessarily meets the definition of theft or one that would give rise to a claim under a standard material damage policy.

Another area where difficulty can arise will be the actions of malicious persons, virus writers clearly falling within such a definition. The standard exclusions with regards the actions of malicious persons (i.e the act of government, actions of strikers/locked out workers etc.) might not in the first instance debar a claim in respect of damage to software in respect of malicious persons not falling within one of those excluded categories. The onus of proving that an exclusion applies would rest with the insurer -

suspicion that an employee may have facilitated the introduction of a virus would be insufficient.

The conclusion of the above comments is that there may be significant exposure (subject to exclusions), particularly in respect of All Risks policies for losses flowing from Damage to software that were not intended initially, either by the insured business or by the insurer. However, as time goes on, the level of general awareness that these issues exist increases, and the failure of any action to confirm any limitation in cover insofar as such new exposures arise might be deemed to be acceptance of them.

Extensions

There are business interruption extensions that do not require satisfaction of the Material Damage Proviso, and claims might be submitted which side step much of the above discussion as a consequence.

The most obvious example is the Denial of Access extension. As noted previously, at the time that the Denial of Access extension was written, it will not have been in the contemplation of the parties for insurance to embrace non-physical Denials of Access. Notwithstanding that, the threat of a Distributed Denial of Service (DDOS) is significant. For either frivolous or criminal intent, small programs might be sent out by miscreants to a variety of personal computers at domestic addresses, all to activate and attempt to contact a particular website at a given time on a given day.

The volume of traffic resulting therefrom is intended to overwhelm the subject website and cause it to crash. This is an issue that has featured in the press recently, youths renting out networks of computers for just that purpose. The customers subsequently attempting to access the site to make a purchase would be unable to do so and a Denial of Access claim might be submitted. In terms of the business suffering such an attack, this is not truly akin to a Denial of Access claim. If the website has been crashed, and if there is a claim to be made, it could only be in respect of Damage to that site rather than access to it. In the same way as a burning factory might not be entered, the public could still visit the perimeter of the demised Premises and look in at the flames. Access to the (perimeter of the) Premises would not be denied.

However, there may be another website which derives the vast majority of its business via a hyperlink button from the website that has crashed.

Depending on the circumstances, that other website might indeed have suffered a Denial of Access, and may feel it appropriate to submit an insurance claim subject to the policy cover. Of course, based upon the suggestion throughout this book that pre claim discussion of the business will avoid surprises, it should not be the case, if the vast majority of turnover is dependent on one feeding website, that this would not have been identified by the insured business previously. If it were the case that the finance director, or insurance buyer, had consistently declined to provide any real detail in respect of the operation of the business, then a sympathetic hearing can hardly be expected when the claim is made.

The Denial of Access extension (or indeed the Loss of Attraction extension) requires an incident to occur in the vicinity/immediate vicinity. Were it to be the case that electronic variations of the perils or extensions are not specifically excluded, then such terms would have to be interpreted insofar as they can be in digital terms. If a website in the United Kingdom is accessed via a hyperlink button from a website in Australia, it could be the case that such a website comprises the electronic vicinity. This might be consistent with that part of the pavement from which customers step to cross the threshold of a shop comprising the vicinity in physical terms.

Another example to consider is the extension relating to Damage flowing from riot or the actions of malicious persons. In the recent case of *Tektrol*, it was decided that the receipt of a virus represented a loss at the hands of a malicious person, whether it was received unintentionally from a friendly source or directly from such a person. The standard Association of British Insurers' wording excludes *'Consequential loss... arising from deliberate erasure loss distortion or corruption of information on computer systems or other records...'*. As this is specifically a business interruption rather than material damage extension, the latter exclusion is supported by the *Tektrol* case.

However, this is a developing area of the law. Should a future decision suggest that 'deliberate' damage to software systems should not be inferred if there is an unintentional introduction of a virus from a regular business partner, then inadvertent cover might arise.

Exclusions

There are two issues to consider in respect of exclusions.

Firstly, there are existing exclusions in respect of perils that have equal application to digital or physical scenarios. Consider the following:

> *A CNC machine downloads software upgrades from the Internet on a regular basis. Apparently obtaining such a download using a password from a verified site, the software patch that is downloaded is in fact infected by a virus which causes the accuracy of the machine cutting head to move out of alignment over a period of time. The problem does not reveal itself until the cutting accuracy falls outside tolerance some weeks after the software was downloaded. Damage to product results, with the loss of the customer's business following.*

It might be argued that the degradation in the software is a gradually arising issue and falls within an existing exclusion. In reality, it might be the case that the cause would never be traced back to the initial download. Matters are always clearer in hypothetical examples than in real life. It is to be hoped that businesses would keep backups such that a reload of a previous version would allow production to continue regardless of such an incident. Of course, if backups ran on a grandfather/father/son basis (i.e. rotating saved copies of three or four disks/reels as appropriate), then it would only be a matter of time before the problem represented itself if it were a case of gradual progression.

With regards to backups, it may be the case that we are moving towards a situation where a failure to take regular effective backups will constitute a lack of reasonable care to the extent of recklessness. It is not uncommon for there to be backup warranties under the material damage sections of existing of policies. These will require regular backups. It is not unusual for there to be a difficulty with such backups and for it to become apparent post claim that they are not tested with any degree of regularity and in fact do not work. Underwriters may be tempted to argue that the requirement to take a backup implies a working and effective backup. A judge might conclude that the decision not to include a simple clause explicitly requiring such backups to be tested for efficacy would make it onerous to infer such a proposition on the part of the insured person.

With regards to the application of an exclusion, the onus of proof lies with insurers. In the case of digital claims, the window of opportunity to investigate circumstances is likely to be very limited. If physical stock is affected by smoke or flood, it can be put to one side of the warehouse for the loss adjuster to examine in due course, and the business can otherwise continue unaffected.

In the case of a virus attack to the operating system, a business will have to attempt to fix the problem as soon as possible, and carry on normal operations to avoid exponential business interruption losses arising. The window of opportunity and the ability to investigate is very much diminished compared with normal claims. In specific situations this might not be the case. If a website is damaged, a screen print might be made showing the nature of the Damage, or a copy retained of what is likely to be relatively defined data for subsequent examination. A pervasive problem, however, affecting many systems, is unlikely to be able to be quarantined in this way and resumption of business at the earliest opportunity will be preferred.

It is desirable as a consequence, if it is intended for digital cover to be provided, for there to be a significant time excess or franchise applicable to the policy. This will avoid any inertia or misunderstandings, given that IT difficulties are likely to arise to a minor extent as a routine part of most businesses. The occurrence of an insured peril can have a paralysing effect on businessmen - the possibility that insurance might be available produces a caution which, if unchecked, can lead to decisions which with the benefit of hindsight may appear to be bizarre. This is the case with all claims, not merely with those relating to digital risk.

The presence of a significant excess/franchise will remove that fear, and will empower relevant employees to press on and rectify difficulties without being concerned that they might inadvertently cause a problem with recovery of funds from insurers. In many cases, the potential insurance proceeds are very minor compared to the losses courted through inactivity.

There is secondly the issue of exclusions applied specifically in terms of digital risks. The difficulty in producing relevant wordings derives from the fact that this is a relatively unproven area and the legal status of some of the terminology is unclear. The term 'worm', for example would generally be understood to constitute something undesirable in IT terms, but it is also a term used to relate to a type of data warehousing. The term 'Trojan Horse' is important to avoid a definition of viruses requiring self replication, but that particular wording is also, at the current time legally untested.

Whether all of the wordings currently in the market place would properly deal with sentinel software that, unbeknown to the victim, steals a little bit of hard disk space as a basecamp to gather information from, subsequently depriving the victim of sole enjoyment of that information (as discussed before whether or not that type of issue constitutes theft in the traditional sense is open to doubt) has yet to be seen.

Some exclusion wordings go so far as to reject any claim for Damage to software, which is a significant reduction in the cover previously available, given that insurers have paid for loss of software in the past. Indeed, the greater the level of detail in which an exclusion is framed, the greater the risk of falling foul of the offside trap and having a judge conclude that if a term does not appear on the detailed list, there must have been a conscious intention to provide cover for it.

Whether or not, given the experience of the millennium bug, the risks are so great that blanket exclusion is required or not remains to be seen. Two practical observations, however, might be offered:

Firstly, limits of indemnity can now be seen in respect of Damage to systems (computer systems) under material damage covers, but there are generally no corresponding limitations in respect of business interruption covers, which is probably where the catastrophic claims will arise.

Secondly, it might be as well to amend the definition of contents such that the decision to provide cover for computer systems, books and records is by specific extension rather than, having granted the coverage, insurers needing to rely on an exclusion.

Ultimately, the intention of the insured business/broker and the insurer will dictate the appropriate approach. There is a possibility, however, that general commercial wordings currently (inadvertently) provide cover, and exclusion wordings may or may not limit the cover to that intended between the parties.

It will be appreciated that the discussion above has mainly been relevant to general commercial policies providing business interruption and material damage cover. There are specialist policies that can be taken out in respect of digital risks, and these may provide a convenient addition where the core policy does not offer the cover. It is likely that the decision to purchase additional cover will reflect detailed pragmatic discussion having taken place. The problem claims are not likely to arise in those cases. Issues will occur when a very significant loss arises, and an attempt is made to pursue a claim that was not within the contemplation of the parties at the relevant time, but in respect of which the policy wording may be imprecise.